The Pomegranate Pendant

by Dvora Waysman

 Mazo Publishers
Jerusalem, Israel

The Pomegranate Pendant

Text Copyright © 2007 Dvora Waysman
ISBN: 978-965-7344-22-4

Published by:

IVI Mazo Publishers
Chaim Mazo, Publisher
P.O. Box 36084   Jerusalem 91360 Israel

Email: info@mazopublishers.com
Website: www.mazopublishers.com
Israel: 054-7294-565
USA: 1-815-301-3559

Credits:
Cover Design – Frumi Mazo
Cover Photo – Flavio Sklar
Jewelry courtesy of Studio Sarah Einstein; Joyce Bennett
Yemenite Headdress (*gargush*) courtesy of
the Zadok family, Jerusalem

About The Author

Dvora Waysman was born Dorothy Opas in Melbourne, Australia. She made *aliyah* with her husband, Zvi, and their four children in 1971 to Israel. She now has 18 Israeli grandchildren.

Today, Dvora makes her home in Jerusalem where she is widely known as a teacher of creative writing. A freelance journalist syndicated worldwide, Dvora is the author of ten books.

In 1981, she was awarded the "For Jerusalem" citation by Mayor Teddy Kollek for her fiction, poetry and features about the city, and in 1988 she received the Seeff Award for Best Foreign Correspondent from the Society for Justice, Ethics and Morals in Journalism.

Dvora has also served as the Press Officer of the Shaare Zedek Medical Center in Jerusalem.

The Pomegranate Pendant is a work of fiction. The ben-Yichyas are not based on any living people, present or past. However, throughout the novel, reference is made to authentic historical figures and the book is set against the backdrop of real events which took place in the years 1882-1956.

Prologue

ONE OF MY BEST CUSTOMERS ever, who was to become also a dear friend, a French-Algerian lady of untold wealth and sophistication, often said:

"Plus ça change, plus ça reste le meme"

(The more things change, the more they stay the same.)

And as I fastened the gold pendant on its slender gold chain around Bracha's neck, the pomegranate pendant that had been mine, and my daughter's, and her daughter's, and her daughter's, I sighed deeply, just as dear Dominique always had when she spoke in her refined way of there being nothing new under the sun. Bracha was so different from the child-bride I had been when the pendant first graced my neck. And yet, in so many important ways, she was the same.

The fine golden pomegranate was almost lost amid all the other jewelry with which Bracha, in accordance with our time-honored custom, was adorned, but my eyes focused only on this delicate pendant.

"Wear it with my blessing," I whispered. "Do you know its meaning?" Bracha cast down her gaze modestly and shook her head. The slight movement stirred the crimson flowers in her headdress. Automatically, I reached up to balance the weighty *gargush*, an unnecessary adjustment as the bride was well-rehearsed in bearing the cumbersome head piece with apparent ease.

"The pomegranate is a fruit blessed with many seeds, my child. So may you be blessed with many children."

Impulsively she kissed me. "I love you, *Savta* Mazal."

My eyes filled with tears of gratitude that the Almighty had spared me and lengthened my days to the age of ninety, to be present at the *Chinah* of my great-great-granddaughter Bracha.

"Look after the pomegranate pendant – it is very special. May you fasten it round your daughter's neck at *her* Chinah ceremony and, with Hashem's help, at her daughter's also."

She laughed, not really understanding how fast the years fly. Well, she was young – only 18 years old – but not nearly as young as I had been when Ezra had given the precious pendant to me at my Chinah in Yemen so long ago.

Part
One

1

I WAS FOURTEEN when Abba called me to his tiny workroom at the back of our house. Our home was not very different from most of the homes of Jews in Sana'a, as many of them too were artisans of one sort or another and they too plied their crafts in small, airless workrooms attached to their houses. But to my eyes, Abba's workshop was an enchanted place. It was like al-Adin's cave, filled with baskets of amber baubles, gold filigree hands to ward off the Evil Eye, coils of gold wire waiting to be worked into necklaces, bracelets and earrings, and silver beads in all different shapes and sizes.

Abba was completing a dowry of exquisite jewelry for the daughter of a wealthy Moslem client. The customer had ordered an unusual necklace of golden cardamom seeds, the Moslem symbol of fertility, and my father had produced a truly outstanding piece. He had also wrought a handsome gold buckle for the bridegroom's belt and silver ornaments for the caparison, the saddle, and the bridle of the fine Arabian steed on which the groom would ride when he came to collect his bride.

"Come to me, my Mazal," Father commanded me.

"Yes, Abba?"

"I have almost finished this order – I will receive a goodly sum," he said with satisfaction. I was happy for him. He worked so hard, and often with little reward. Yemen was then ruled not by one but two competing imams, and they both taxed the Jews heavily and issued more and more oppressive decrees, so that no matter how hard their Jewish subjects worked, they could not really prosper.

My father was no exception.

"Do you like Ezra?" Father asked me suddenly. "Ezra ben-Yichya, your apprentice?"

"How many eligible Ezras do you know?" Abba chuckled.

I blushed. I really did not know any boys except my brothers, but of course I saw Ezra every day when I brought a finjan of *gisher* to the shop for them to sip as they worked, its ginger and cinnamon spices filling the air with a refreshing tang. "I like him well enough," I replied softly, not raising my eyes.

"Well enough to marry him?" my father asked gently.

I did not know what to say. I had turned fourteen two months earlier and many of my friends were already married – my best friend Yifat Yemeni was a mother, and she was only 13.

"He is a good boy from a fine family," Abba added. I knew that Ezra's father, who made tools for the Moslem farmers, was a pious man who learned well into the night with my father, and that Ezra, with his long, curly payot and serious expression, also spent many hours studying the holy books after he finished his day's work as a goldsmith.

Still I remained silent.

My father took my hands in his. "So, my Mazal?"

"I have never spoken to him, Abba."

"Of course you have not. But he has spoken to me. He wants your hand in marriage. Do you object?"

I shook my head. I felt strange – excited and afraid at the same time. He was a good boy, as my father had said; quiet and polite, not rough like some of the boys of Sana'a. And he was handsome – hair as black as jet and eyes like glowing coals.

My father nodded, satisfied. "I will be paid in a few days for this commission, and then we will have the week of your Chinah."

"So soon?" I cried, alarmed.

"It is time, my daughter. Ezra has learned the craft well, and he has his own tools. I want you to go with him to the Promised Land, to welcome the Redeemer."

Suddenly I understood the conversations of the elders, which always ceased when I or my young friends came into the room. It had begun with the visit of Tov el-Nadaf, who had actually seen Jerusalem with his own eyes and said that the Messiah was soon coming. Since then, there had been no other subject discussed by my parents and their neighbors. I was afraid. "Will you and Imma come with us?"

Father shook his head sadly. "I cannot leave – the Arab masters will not let me go."

"Why not?" I began to tremble. Tears filled my eyes but I would not allow myself to cry and appear childish.

"They have decreed that any artisan who chooses to emigrate must first train a Moslem apprentice to replace him, and that will take years – they have no skill at this delicate filigree work. But if we were all to leave, the masters fear there will be no one to fashion their jewelry, to embroider their robes, to weave their baskets, to chisel stone pots and forge their scythes. So, until they are satisfied, the best of the craftsmen must stay."

"And you are the best, Abba," I cried, flinging myself to the ground at his feet.

Tenderly, he smoothed my hair. "I have taught Ezra well," Father said. "He is a good goldsmith. He will look after you, and one day your mother and I will come too. You will prepare a place for us in Jerusalem." As he said the name of the Holy City, his eyes shone. "Now go, my daughter. I must finish my work. Go to your mother – she will arrange everything for your wedding. Do you want to speak to Ezra when he comes tomorrow?"

I was overcome with shyness. "Must I?"

"No, my child. It is enough that you spoke to me. I will tell him the good news. When you are his wife, you will have much to say – too much, just like your mother!" he laughed warmly.

And just as he had said, only a week later I had my Chinah ceremony, to honor the bride and groom and give each of us to the other's family.

On the day of the ceremony, my mother dressed me lovingly in the very clothing and jewels she had worn at her Chinah. We stood in the tiny room I shared with my four younger sisters, trembling as my mother took four cloth squares and wrapped them neatly around my neck. Then she helped me dress in a caftan woven of golden thread, with embroidered leggings. Over this came layers of gold and silver filigree necklaces, and next, the high, conical *gargush*, a headdress adorned with gold, silver and pearls. Fresh flowers framed the tall cone, and bunches of fragrant mint hung from my ears.

All the women of the community assembled in the courtyard of our house, and as we came out the women began to ululate, clicking their tongues in a high-pitched wail to frighten away the evil spirits. Then the music began – a throbbing rhythm that my old Aunt Miriam beat out with a wooden stick against a large tambour drum, while my little sister Odaya banged on the lid of a pot with a spoon. All the family chanted wedding songs and prayers in our special Hebrew-Arabic language as my Ezra came to meet me at the door.

"I have a gift for you, Mazal," Ezra said softly. Only

I could hear him above the din. "I made it myself – I hope you like it." He opened his hand and nestling in the palm was an exquisite gold filigree pomegranate suspended from a slender gold chain. The workmanship was astonishing.

I was too overcome with emotion to speak. I had watched my father at work for enough years to know how much time and skill had gone into its making, and I could picture Ezra seated cross-legged on his straw mat, shaping the delicate pomegranate from the fine gold wires that gave the filigree pendant its lacy appearance. I added it to all the other necklaces I was wearing, yet somehow I was aware only of it, as though it glittered more brightly than the rest.

I followed him to a table strewn with flowers. The perfume of the jasmine on the night air was intoxicating. The table was covered with large platters of wonderful food, and my aunt was ladling out heaping platefuls of spicy shaweeya for all the guests. Everyone sang and danced for hours (and I did too, despite the weight of my adornments), until my mother summoned them to silence by beating on the cymbals. She came towards us with the *mazbera* bowl containing a concoction made from the ground-up seeds and leaves of the henna plant, mixed with water and heated until it resembled an orange/brown mud.

My mother recited a prayer in our honor. Then she made a circle of henna on Ezra's palm, explaining that it was symbolic of a seal on his hand and his heart. He was now going to his bride and she would always be a blessed and honored member of his family. Imma then blessed me, putting a dab of henna on my hand and repeated the procedure with Ezra's parents and his brothers and sisters as well as mine.

Everyone became quiet as Imma and Ezra's mother led me to the *chupah*. We stood facing Eretz Yisrael. This was the most solemn part of the wedding: the *kiddushin*. After the reading of the *ketubah*, six of my father's friends from the synagogue were invited to read the benedictions after our *Mori* had blessed the wine. Then, in memory of the destruction of the Temple, Ezra broke the wine glass – we were now man and wife. My mother had prepared a small meal for us to eat alone – we were both too shy to talk – before we rejoined the guests for the first festive meal.

Finally, it was over and we entered the small house where we would live together for the next few months. Ezra looked at the henna circles on my hands and, in the words of King Solomon, said, "My beloved is a cluster of henna in the vineyards of Ein Gedi." My heart swelled with joy.

Unconsciously, my fingers found the pomegranate pendant that hung around my neck. I felt it would forever be my most treasured possession, because my husband had created it as a gift for our wedding day.

"Do you like it, Mazal?"

I nodded, meeting his eyes for the first time. "I will wear it always," I assured him softly. No matter how much or how little we would take with us when the time came to depart for the Holy Land, no matter what jewelry I might have at any other time in my life, my beautiful pomegranate necklace would remain closest to my heart.

2

OUR DEPARTURE from Sana'a was set for *Elul*. It was the year 5641 by our calendar, although our official travel documents were inscribed with the date of August 1881. We had only been married a short time and soon our dream of settling in the Holy City would come true. We wanted to leave Sana'a just after the fast of Tishah b'Av, to allow enough time for us to arrive before Rosh Hashanah – a new year, a new beginning.

The timing was important: we were fulfilling our destiny and we needed to reach holy soil by 5642. Our *Chachamim* had taught that 642 was the numerical equivalent of *b'tamar* – the word in the Torah verse that signaled the time for the Redemption.

In truth, everyone from the community wanted to make the pilgrimage, but many did not qualify. Some, like my father, were skilled artisans and were not permitted to emigrate. Others were too old, or had small babies who might not survive the difficult journey.

Two years earlier there had been a dreadful epidemic of typhus in the *chart el-Yahud,* the Jewish Quarter of Sana'a. Before the plague, we had numbered 30,000, but after, there were a mere 12,000 – may they be shielded from the Evil Eye and may they be fruitful and multiply. Our family had been spared, praise God. I think it had much to do with my mother's wonderful herbal remedies that she always administered to us at the first sign of any illness. She promised to teach me everything she knew before we left – everything she was taught by her mother, who had been taught by her mother – and to give me seeds and seedlings to take with me to our new life.

There was so much for me to learn, and so little time to learn it! Girls my age in Sana'a were of course well-trained in housekeeping duties by the time they were wed, and quite naturally my friends and I helped tend our younger sisters and brothers, so child-rearing was not strange to us either. But it was accepted that when we married we would live in the household of our husband's family, where his mother would always be on hand to guide us in our new role. I was not to have this advantage.

And so, until the time of our departure, I kept house for Ezra – cooking, cleaning, embroidering and weaving – and spent many hours being taught by my mother all the skills I would need. Although she had never had any schooling, she was terribly wise. Her garden was filled with herbs and spices that she would add to our food to make it savory and fragrant, or pulverize or steep to produce medicines and poultices with which to treat our ailments.

Now she showed me each plant and explained its medicinal properties. "This is *reichan* – basil. See what pretty leaves it has, Mazal?"

"It smells good too, Imma."

"That is why the Master of the World created it, my daughter. If you crush the dried leaves and use them like snuff, reichan will help you to breathe more easily when you have a cold. It is a good remedy for headaches, too. When your father feels poorly, I soak the leaves in wine to make a tonic, and also..." she looked at me questioningly "it helps bring the milk for feeding the babies?"

I blushed bright red. "Not yet, Imma," I whispered, although we were all alone in the garden. Such talk was not for men's ears.

"Perhaps it is just as well. You have a long journey ahead and the way might be hard." She pointed to a graceful herb I recognized as one that she always added to soup. I knew it was delicate-flavored and the thick green leaves were especially tasty. "This one cleanses your blood and helps you digest your food. It makes you perspire, so use it for fevers. It will also take away bruises and relieve painful joints."

As we circled the garden, I felt the familiar plant names returning to me like an unused language – I'd been helping Imma with her remedies ever since I could walk but, like all children, I had never really listened to her explanations on a conscious level. Now they were coming back to me and I realized that I too loved the plants which she nurtured so tenderly.

"What is this, Mazal?"

"It's *hel* – cardamom, Imma. Abba makes jewelry in its likeness for the Moslems."

She nodded. "And this?" She pointed to a large fragrant shrub. "I don't know, Imma."

"It's *chasa el-ban* – rosemary. It strengthens your heart, so it is good to use it even if you are not ill."

Round and round the garden we went, and although it was by no means a neatly sculpted ornamental garden like the one I had once seen when I peeked over the wall of a rich Arab's mansion, there was a special orderliness to everything. As Imma's explanations continued, the entire garden seemed to take on structure and precision. Certain plants could not thrive alongside others; some required shade and huddled beneath the broad leaves of larger shrubs that loved the sun. Soon I knew all that she could teach me, and I felt blessed to have such a clever mother.

Every night Ezra attended meetings at the synagogue to plan the trip to Jerusalem. I was sad to be leaving my family and fearful of what lay ahead, but my father gave us courage. He believed we would be redeemed when we reached the Holy City, and now we believed that too.

There were several hundred of us who planned to go together, and the discussions were endless. Those who had homes tried to sell them, but it was almost impossible because Moslems did not want to live in the *chart el-Yahud* and none of the Jews who remained could possibly afford to buy. Those who had to stay behind wept bitterly; we all prayed that they would soon be able to follow us.

At last, the plans were finalized: we were to travel on foot to Aden and then by ship to Port Said. From there, we'd take the railway to Jaffa, and go on to Jerusalem by donkey.

With such a journey ahead of us, we could not take much with us, but we did not think that we would need a lot. We had heard that the Sultan of Turkey was allowing Jews to settle in Jerusalem – Palestine, of course, was part of his empire, so he could decree as he pleased; for the time being, he was in a generous mood concerning Jewish settlement. Also, there were rumors that a rich Jewish baron known as "Rashil" was buying land outside the Old City walls and giving it away to Jews willing to live there. So we took the little money we had from my dowry and some jewelry my father gave me, and Ezra packed all his artisan's tools that he would need to work in the Holy Land. We also took our holy books and ritual objects, our clothes, and as many herbs as my mother could press on me.

On the morning of our departure, the sun shone brightly in a cloudless blue sky and all the Jews of Sana'a came to bid us farewell and give us their blessing.

Although I was married and expected to behave like a grown woman, I still felt like a little girl and wept as I embraced my parents.

"Do not be afraid, Mazal," my father said, his own eyes full of tears. "Ezra will take care of you. It will be good. It is written: 'And I will rejoice in Jerusalem and delight in My people; never again shall be heard there the sound of weeping and the sound of wailing. And they shall build houses and inhabit them; and they shall plant vineyards and eat the fruit of them.' The words of the prophet will be fulfilled in your days, God willing."

"I wish you could come too – all of you," I sobbed, as I looked at my brothers and sisters clustered around my parents like pale amber beads encircling two precious jewels.

"Soon – soon – be brave, my daughter. Be a woman of valor," my mother whispered. They waved until we were out of sight. Somehow I felt comforted by the last words my mother had said to me. I would be an *eshet chayil* and make a new life with my husband. And one day we would all be together again, in Jerusalem.

3

IT WAS A VERY hard journey – much harder than anything I could have imagined. It's not that we were unaccustomed to walking, as few families owned their own donkeys or wagons, but none of us had ever gone such a long distance on foot. There were 250 of us when we started out, yet less than one hundred reached Aden; many had dropped out along the way and returned to Sana'a. I had been too ashamed to say so, but I also had wanted to return. My feet ached and the pack on my back grew heavier with every step.

Ezra sensed my suffering. To lift my spirits he encouraged me with stories of what it would be like when we reached Jerusalem.

"It will be gold and silver, like my jewelry," he said. "Golden in the sunshine and silver in the moonlight."

"How can you know that, Ezra?" I was petulant and unwilling to be placated.

"It is written, Mazal. Always the Prophets have praised the beauty of the Holy City, and the Sages teach that ten measures of beauty were given to the world, and nine of them were taken by Jerusalem."

I believed him, but his words did not relieve my pains. His yearning for Jerusalem, however, was strong enough for two, and so, although he was already carrying double my load, he took more of the parcels from me. I was glad my father had chosen Ezra – many of the husbands had become angry with their wives complaining, and this resulted in loud arguments unlike anything I had ever heard at home. Ezra's gentleness and patience with me made me feel ashamed and I tried to make amends.

"Tell me again how it will be in Jerusalem," I pleaded, forcing a smile to my lips. I really did need the reassurance, for the longing for my family left behind was always with me.

Ezra's eyes shone. "Jerusalem is a jewel – King David's city. My father told me that many, many generations back, my forefathers made sacred vessels and ornaments for the Holy Temple, may it be rebuilt in our days. And utensils for the High Priest. Each father passed on his goldsmithing skills to his son, until this very day. We must continue to hone our skill and improve our craft so that we will be ready for the day when we are once again called upon for this glorious undertaking."

"Tell me more about Jerusalem," I persisted. Although I knew that Ezra had never been there either, he was so wise and knew so much more than me. As always, my husband was very patient with me.

"It was King David's city for 400 years," he explained, "until the Babylonians conquered it, and we were dispersed. We wept with longing for our beautiful city, and for the magnificent dwelling place of the Holy One that their king Nevuchadnetzar destroyed."

I looked at him with admiration. "How do you know all this, Ezra?"

"It is written," he assured me. "The Persian King Cyrus allowed our people to return and build a second Temple, but that was also destroyed."

"So what will we find in Jerusalem? Is our Holy City a ruins?"

He looked nonplused. "Soon, Mazal, we will see it with our own eyes. I am sure it is the most beautiful sight in the world." After many days – so many I lost count – we reached the port city of Aden. It was situated right on the equator and the heat was intense, unbearable. We had been told to search for the family of the merchant Madmur ibn Bundar, the head of the Jewish community, who would help us. The Jews of Aden were different from our people in Sana'a, although many of them were also goldsmiths, weavers, masons, and armorers. We were told that the new Canal of Suez, which had opened only 15 years earlier, brought many foreigners to their city. The Jews of Aden mixed freely with these foreigners and learned their modern ways, so they were more worldly than our people in Sana'a. Still, they were kind to us and gave us food and shelter until the ship came to take us to the Holy Land.

I had never seen such a ship, and I was terrified. Like most of the women, and some of the men, I cried and vowed I would not go aboard – I would not believe that a boat of steel could take us safely to our destination. Like Pharaoh's chariots at the Red Sea, the vessel would sink to the bottom and the waters would close over us. We would drown.

For the first time since our marriage, Ezra became angry with me. "Where is your *bitachon*?" he chastised me. "Do you think the Holy One would let us founder when we are going on a pilgrimage? It is a mitzvah to settle in Eretz Yisrael and those engaged in a mitzvah have Divine protection from all harm."

I followed him up the gangplank without another word. Yifat, my friend, was close behind me with her husband Reuven and her baby Evyatar. The baby was gurgling, his fat little fists beating the air, and I felt ashamed of my own childishness. But when the big engines started to throb, again I was overcome with fear.

I was not alone – men as well as women clung to the ships rails, their eyes glued to the waters that were being churned up violently. Our friends in Aden stood on the dock waving to us as the boat pulled away from the shore, and I thought to myself: the wandering Jews again uprooted, only this time we had a true destination. We were traveling to our homeland.

The ship took us to Port Said in Egypt, and we were all afraid, for this was the land where Israel had been enslaved... Every year at Pesach, we retold the story inscribed in Abba's Haggadah. But the only harassment we suffered came from small trading boats that gathered in the harbor to meet us. Merchants actually climbed aboard our ship, wanting to sell us all kinds of leather goods and trinkets. I saw a bag that I truly fancied, made from strips of different colored leather plaited together, but Ezra said we must save our money for Jerusalem. I knew he was right and I didn't persist, but I was very disappointed.

We were anxious to reach the Holy Land, so the very day we disembarked, we boarded the railway train to Jaffa. All the traveling had left me feeling terribly unwell, and several times I was actually sick.

Our group completely filled the train, with the women of course all seated together at the back of each carriage. I was glad to find myself alongside Yifat. In Sana'a we had lived in the same street until she got married, and it seemed like such a short time ago that we were little girls playing together, running and laughing in the garden, our hair streaming in the wind. Although she was younger than me by a year, I'd always felt I could ask her for advice, and this was especially so since she became a married woman. She was wed at twelve, but we had remained close friends, even after Evyatar was born and the gap between us widened. I loved playing with Evyatar, who was now asleep in her arms, one thumb in his mouth and his soft cheek nestled against his mother's shoulder.

"The traveling is too hard for me, Yifat," I complained. "I am not brave like you."

"We will soon be there, Mazal. Take heart. When we reach Jaffa, there will be donkeys waiting for us and then it will be only two days' ride to Jerusalem."

"Aren't you afraid?"

She nodded. "A little bit. But Reuven said when we reach Jerusalem, Mashiach will come and we will be redeemed."

"What does that mean, exactly?" I asked her.

She was silent for a while. "I'm not sure. But it will be good. You'll be happy, Mazal."

I began to weep. "I feel sick all the time."

She looked at me shrewdly.

"I don't think it is the journey that is causing your sickness, my friend."

"Not the plague!?" I cried out, frightened. "Not the typhus!?"

Yifat laughed. "No, no. I think it is a good sickness."

"How can a sickness be good?" I asked, completely baffled.

She took my hand and placed it on her baby's head. His black curls were like satin.

"Evyatar was my good sickness. I was sick all the time too, in the beginning."

My eyes widened. "Do you think...?"

She smiled at me and, although I still felt queasy, I was suffused with joy. I took Evyatar in my arms and felt his warm little body. Suddenly I knew she was right. I wanted to tell Ezra, and my parents, and my brothers and sisters. The rumble of the train that had given me such a headache now sounded like music. Yifat gave my hand a gentle squeeze and we smiled at each other.

A new land, a new beginning...and a new life!

4

WE DISEMBARKED IN JAFFA, and I saw many of the older people prostrate themselves and kiss the ground. "The Holy Land!" they cried in rapture, while I only looked around in bewilderment. The port was exotic and strange: fishermen were bringing in their daily catch; there was a cluster of large black rocks in the water; ships and fishing boats of different sizes and colors bobbled near the docks. At a little open-air cafe on the wharf, men were sipping Turkish coffee and eating sweet pastries – baklava and ziabiya – similar to those my mother made. Some of the men milling about wore flat-topped hats with tassels dangling, while others wore Moslem robes and head scarves, and still others were in western attire. Even among this peculiar mixture I felt our group stood out and attracted curious stares. I could see jutting above the stone houses of the city the outline of mosques and minarets like those we had left in Yemen.

"This Palestine..." I whispered to Ezra, "it doesn't look very Jewish." Ezra motioned me to be quiet, but I could see that he was also puzzled.

We bought some oranges at an open stand, a kiosk that sold many kinds of food. Although we were hungry, we could not trust the food to be *kasher,* so we managed with the fruits we had seen for the first time at Port Said, and then followed the others to the part of town where the donkeys were waiting for us. I had not had a chance to tell Ezra my happy suspicion about the "sickness" that had plagued me throughout the journey, but I think he may have already guessed. He helped me to mount the donkey, unusually solicitous of my comfort.

It was to be a two-day ride to Jerusalem and a guide rode in front to lead the way. The roads were rocky, even treacherous in many parts, and several times my donkey stumbled, nearly pitching me off. The sun was hot. There were very few trees, I noticed, and I wondered why until I heard the guide explain to one of the men that the Pasha of Egypt, Muchammed Ali, who had ruled over Palestine forty years earlier, had cut down a great many of the trees to build his naval fleet, leaving much of the center of the country denuded of all foliage.

Eventually we reached the city of Ramle where we would spend the night. I wanted to tell Ezra that it also looked like a Moslem city, but I thought he'd be angry with me. However, after he went with the men to talk to the guide, he came back and reported what he had learned.

"It is a Moslem town, Mazal – the only one in Palestine that the Moslems themselves built."

"So why must we tarry here? The Moslems despise us!"

"It is too far for the donkeys to go all the way to Jerusalem without a rest. The guide assures us we are safe, so you needn't worry. Jews live here too – Jews from North Africa – and we will stay in their part of town. Ramle was built by Suleiman the Magnificent, the sultan who built the gates and walls of the Holy City."

"Why did he build it?" I always wanted to learn new things, but girls did not go to school in Yemen. I had been able to teach myself many skills because my father had always indulged me in this regard; it was my tremendous good fortune that Ezra had patience for me too. "It had a good position," my husband explained. "The city is on the south-to-north route from Egypt to Syria and on the west-to-east route from the coast inland. The Crusaders camped here and so did Napoleon."

The names meant nothing to me, yet I liked to listen to Ezra talk. He did not laugh at my questions or brush me aside as many husbands did. Each day I felt more grateful to my father for choosing Ezra for me. My mother had wanted me to marry Avraham Hamarati, the son of the *Chacham,* because it would have brought great pride and honor to the family, but my father had been training Ezra in goldsmithing for three years and knew him well. I suppose he recognized that Ezra's gentle nature would balance my impetuous one and that he would have the patience to tolerate my insatiable thirst for knowledge, a trait considered unseemly in a girl in our tradition.

Although Ezra continued to reassure me that we were now in the Holy Land, I felt very uneasy in Ramle and glad when morning came and we could resume our journey to Jerusalem. The men had done a deal during the night and, in addition to the donkeys, there were now some carts. Although I was one of the youngest, Ezra had secured a place for me, no doubt hinting to the elders about my delicate condition. No one questioned me when I clambered on board one of the flatbed carts. I offered to take Yifat's Evyatar on my lap and she handed him over gratefully. I felt a glow of happiness as the child nestled against me. Somehow, holding the baby lessened the pangs of loneliness I suffered for the family I had left behind.

The cart was fitted with wooden plank benches, certainly not luxurious but more comfortable than sitting astride a donkey. Opposite me was seated Suleiman Alsheich, who was one of the *Chachamim* – a friend of my late grandfather's and of *Chacham* Bashi, the Chief Rabbi of Yemen. Suleiman Alsheich was about eighty-five years of age, with a long beard and sidecurls, and was renowned for his piety and wisdom. Throughout the entire trip he repeatedly consulted a book of maps, and became very excited when the places we traversed corresponded to those he located in his book. When we passed Tel Gezer, he told us that it was the place where Yehoshua bin Nun had led the Children of Israel to victory over the Canaanite kings, including the king of Gezer, and that it had come under Israelite rule only when King Solomon received it as a dowry from an Egyptian princess he had wed.

Soon we entered the Valley of Ayalon, a sweeping plain of emerald green vegetation. This was the main route leading to the Judean hills and even I began to get excited. The wise man told us this was the battleground where Yehoshua had bidden the sun to stand still, and where Yehudah the Maccabee had defeated the Greeks as he battled his way through to Jerusalem.

We crossed a narrow bridge to the Latrun monastery and continued straight ahead. Suleiman Alsheich following our progress with his finger on the map, and I peeked over his shoulder to see. Such unseemly behavior! But I could not help myself. Soon we were turning past craggy rocks and dangerous curves and entering the narrow pass through the mountains – his map gave it the Arabic name of Bab el-Wad. (I had taught myself to read, with surreptitious help from my father. Ezra did not know of it – nor did my mother, who surely would not have approved.)

The road continued to wind and climb through the Judean hills. There were now wonderful forests of pine that cast welcome shade. We passed another Arab village called Abu Ghosh, and Suleiman Alsheich said that in Biblical times it was known as Kiryat Ye'arim, the site where the Holy Ark rested for twenty years until King David brought it to Jerusalem. The road skirted the village and began a steep descent. I clutched Evyatar tightly, becoming afraid as the wheels spun faster and faster, but it became less steep as we passed the ancient oak forest of Aqua Bella and the ruins of the Crusader fortress called Castel, dominating a hill on the right. Soon, looking upward, we could see the approach to Jerusalem – the Holy City.

At this point, Suleiman Alsheich asked the driver of our cart to stop and to help him down. I thought he must be feeling ill, yet there was such excitement in his eyes.

"I must be the first!" he shouted in a quavering voice. "Let me be the first to see Jerusalem."

Ezra led him to the front of the caravan, which had halted at his shouts. With great difficulty, he mounted a donkey alongside the guide.

Dusk was falling as we approached the towering walls and gates of the Old City. We came up to the Chevron Gate, and just as we reached it, Suleiman cried out: *"Shema Yisrael* – Hear, O Israel! The Lord is our God..." In horror we watched as he slid off his donkey and collapsed on the ground.

The excitement had been too much for him – our revered Suleiman Alsheich was dead. Instead of arriving with shouts of joy, our caravan's first act in the Holy City of Jerusalem, the place of our redemption, was to prepare Suleiman Alsheich's body for burial on the Mount of Olives.

5

IT WAS ON THE EVE of
Rosh Hashanah, in the Hebrew year of
5642, that we reached Jerusalem. The death
of our elder had saddened us but nothing could
still the excitement that stirred within us all at having
arrived at long last.

All through the journey Ezra had encouraged me by
describing the "Jerusalem of Gold" that we would soon
see, and he had assured me that we would receive a
wonderful welcome from our Jewish brethren there. I, in
my childish way, had formed an image in my mind of a
fantasy city, a gleaming, gilded city, each building
glittering like the highly polished pieces of jewelry my
father made, but now that image shattered as I looked
around Jerusalem in the fading light. It looked a primitive
town, more primitive even than Sana'a, and nothing like
bustling Port Said. There were paved streets, but the
paving stones were ancient and cracked) and few people
were about although the hour was not that late. The city
lay within massive stone walls breached by gates that
were locked at nightfall) apparently to keep out bandits.

Tired and weary, we all trudged through the market
area until we reached the Jewish streets, the section we
were told was called the Rova. Some men approached us
and looked us over. "Who are you?" they demanded. So
much for a wonderful welcome, I thought. "We are Jews
who have come to settle in Jerusalem," Ezra replied.

More men joined the group. They were all pale-
skinned and dressed in black frock coats and trousers,

while we were clad in our traditional flowing robes that we had worn in Yemen.

"How can you be Jews?" the Jerusalemites asked suspiciously, addressing us in oddly accented Arabic. "You dress like Arabs!"

Who were *they* to be calling us Arabs! I wondered indignantly. I had never seen any Jews – or anyone else, for that matter – dressed as *they* were.

"We come from Yemen – on the Arabian peninsula," Ezra explained in his calm, quiet way. "This is how we dress there."

"But you have such dark skin. And you even speak like Arabs."

I started to cry. Had we come all this way to be insulted and rejected by our fellow Jews?

Ezra stepped forward. I could see that he was angry, but he maintained his composure and smiled in an open, friendly fashion. "Do you want proof?" he asked. "Would you care to see my *tallit* and *tefillin?*"

"He could have stolen them from Jews!" one man said accusingly.

Ezra was unshaken. He must have realized that to these people we did indeed look different and naturally aroused their suspicion. He began to recite by heart a passage from the Talmud which I did not understand, but these men clearly did.

After a minute or two, the man who seemed to be spokesman for the Jerusalemites raised his hand to halt the flow of Ezra's words of Torah. In Hebrew he said, "We are sorry. Please accept our apology and know that you are welcome." He introduced himself as Rav Porush and one of the others as Rav Blau. I didn't catch the rest of the names. "You must understand," he said, "most of the Jews of the *Yishuv* are of European descent, although of course our ancestors came from the Holy Land many generations ago. We have never before seen Yemenite Jews, but I for one have heard of your community's existence. You look like Arabs – pardon me – so we had good reason to be cautious. Please follow us and we will help you to get settled."

They took us to the study hall of the Churvat Rabi Yehudah He-Chasid synagogue. We could hear some of them talking among themselves, wondering if we were members of one of the "ten lost tribes" who were known to be dark-skinned. One fellow mentioned *Iggeret Teiman*, the famous letter written by the Rambam to the Jews of Yemen, and the other men nodded their agreement.

Word of our arrival quickly got around, and soon a stream of women arrived, each carrying a steaming pot of food. They were very kind to us and I began to feel better. One of the women, who looked like a pale version of my mother, took Yifat's baby in her arms, and kissed him and sang him a lullaby in a language she said was called Yiddish. She told me her name was Sarah. It was most peculiar: I had never heard the language before, but I could sense its meaning. She smiled at me and clasped my hand.

"You are so young – just a child!" she said.

"Oh no!" I corrected her. "I am fourteen. I am a married woman, and soon I will be a mother like Yifat."

Sarah bent and kissed my cheek. "I will be your friend," she said softly, and I wanted to enfold myself in her ample embrace. Suddenly I felt like a little girl longing for her mother.

She noticed my pomegranate pendant and touched it gently with one finger. "What a beautiful necklace!"

"My husband made it for me," I said proudly, pointing to Ezra. "He makes the most beautiful jewelry in the world."

"Is it real gold?"

"Of course," I replied. "He only works with the best quality gold and silver. The finer the metal, the finer the jewelry."

"But who will buy his wares?" Sarah asked.

I looked at her questioningly, not understanding.

She regarded me sadly. "Our community is very poor, my dear. Rich in Torah but poor in means. We struggle to buy food and clothing for our families. We have no money for jewelry."

Tears sprang to my eyes. "Rich Moslems, perhaps?"

Sarah shook her head. "The Arabs have even less than we do. But don't worry; Hashem will provide."

Ezra had not heard this conversation. I was glad – it was too soon to have all his dreams shattered. And I was so tired, I just wanted to sleep. Maybe the new day would bring new solutions. Surely the Almighty would not abandon us at the start of a New Year, in a new land, when we had traveled so far with such hopes.

We continued to sleep in the study hall of the Churvah synagogue until after Yom Kippur. The residents of the Rova invited us to their already overcrowded homes for meals or brought us food to the courtyard. The food was strange to us; it had none of the flavor we were used to from the herbs and spices of our homeland. There was watery chicken soup with just a few pieces of onion or carrot floating in it; unseasoned boiled chicken, white and unappetizing; and tea flavored only with lemon.

When I remarked on the poor quality of the food, Ezra reminded me of how the Children of Israel wandering in the desert after being freed from slavery had complained to Moshe *Rabbeinu* that they missed the leeks and cucumbers and fish of Egypt – spurning the manna which the Almighty in His goodness had sent to feed them. After that, I accepted the Jerusalemites' generous gifts gratefully and graciously, although I still determined that when I had my own home, I would prepare meals like the ones my mother had served.

At the time of our arrival, Jerusalem was bursting at the seams: within its walls lived 22,000 people, of whom 11,000 were Jews, 6,500 were Moslems, and the rest were Christians. It was so crowded that twenty years earlier, a new neighborhood called Mishkenot Sha'ananim (meaning "peaceful dwelling places") had been built by Sir Moses Montefiore, so we were told, a great Jewish philanthropist, with funds donated by his American friend, Yehudah Touro. I knew nothing of these people with unpronounceable names from places I had never heard of. Again Ezra surprised me, explaining everything patiently. He had a book of maps, Suleiman Alsheich's book, and he showed me where these places were, and told me all about the rich Jews whose money helped to build the Holy Land.

Because of the overcrowding I had seen in the Rova, I was anxious to visit Mishkenot Sha'ananim and to try our luck at finding housing there. Early one morning, just after the gates of the city were opened, we were taken to see the new neighborhood.

It was indeed very beautiful – one long, low building which stretched along the slopes to the west of the Old City, and from the garden we had a magnificent view of its parapets, domes and towers. When we turned around, we were awarded a breathtaking vista of the hills leading to the Judean desert beyond.

"Is it safe to live here?" Yifat asked.

The guide who had taken us there was hesitant. "Sometimes there are bandits – but you can always come back at night and we will take you in and lock the gate," he offered.

After the tight security we had seen in the Old City, with guards at the massive gates and the feeling of safety the surrounding walls generated, Mishkenot Sha'ananim seemed terribly vulnerable. Yifat clutched her baby tighter. "So why live here at all?" she asked in her direct, practical way, voicing the concern of all of us.

So we left the new neighborhood to those who were braver than we, and eventually found three tiny rooms in a narrow valley near the Ashpot Gate. This was not one of Jerusalem's beautiful gates – the other seven were far more ornate and artistically hewn. Facing south, it was more of a "back door" to the city than a monument like the others. The little house had one advantage, though: it had a small garden where I could plant my herbs, and that was the first thing I did, even before unpacking our meager belongings and trying to clean the dilapidated rooms.

"We can take our meals in this room," I told Ezra, trying to make the best of it.

He shook his head, "No, Mazal," he said gently.

"But there is a bedroom and a sitting room, and the room that is meant to be a kitchen can be for eating." Why the Ashkenazi ladies liked to cook inside the house was beyond me. I would have no need for an indoor kitchen.

"And where will I work and sell my jewelry, if the baby is to have a room of his own? I must earn a living."

I colored with embarrassment. Sometimes I was so foolish! I hated myself for it and, at the same time, marveled that Ezra never became angry with me, despite my silliness and ignorance.

"Y-yes, of course," I stammered. "The front room –

the best room – that must be your workshop, and the kitchen will be our sitting room."

"Things will get better, Mazal," he assured me. "One day, with the Almighty's help, we will have a fine house with many rooms. When they see my beautiful work, they will flock to buy it and we will be rich."

I swallowed hard. "Ezra, Sarah told me that the Jews are very poor. They do not have any money for gold jewelry."

"So I will work in silver." He looked at me searchingly. "Not for silver either?"

I shook my head miserably.

"So it will be as in Sana'a. I shall have to sell to the rich Moslems."

I hated my task, but I had to tell him what I had learned. "They are not rich, Ezra. They are poorer than the Jews. They have ten, fifteen children. They can't feed them, they can't even send them to school."

He was silent for a while. "People need jewelry, Mazal. They need adornments to brighten sad lives. There were Jewish goldsmiths in Yemen for 2,000 years, making wonderful items in filigree and plaited silver and gold. But even jewelry made from stones, glass, metal and beads adds something beautiful to a life. Torah crowns and mezuzah cases are always in demand, and I can fashion them cheaply. I can make inexpensive jewelry too... I will find a way."

My heart overflowed with love for my husband, who though only a few years older than me had such courage. I was easily frightened, like a child, and easily discouraged, but he had the bravery of a man.

I spent the next weeks scrubbing down the house until the beige stones gleamed. There were natural shelves formed by the stone ledges under the windows and here I arranged the pots I had brought from Yemen. My father had carved them from soapstone, which was highly prized for its halachic purity. There were also some eating bowls. Soapstone is easy to carve and it hardens in the sun. My mother had many such pots for making clarified butter and porridge, and others for wonderful Shabbat meals. I had only three, which I set on the windowsill along with the four bowls and started to sing as I went about my work.

It was true, what Sarah had said: no one had money to buy our jewelry. But Ezra had the clever idea of trading some for the goods we needed. He would come home after his forays with some cushions and sleeping pallets, and a stove to heat the room in winter which I could also use to cook. Jerusalem was much colder than Sana'a had ever been, and when the rains came right after Sukkot, cooking outdoors became impossible. The new stove was made of copper and we filled it with coal.

One day Ezra came home with a table from Damascus, inlaid with mother-of-pearl. It was the most beautiful piece I'd even seen. I had some old hessian sacking on which I embroidered a picture of the Western Wall with some colored wool my new friend Sarah gave me, and this now decorated one wall of the room. On another wall, I put up my treasured silk-embroidered shawl – my mother had given it to me when we left Sana'a. It was turquoise and lavender, pale pink and purple. Its brightness concealed the dingy plastered stone. My depression lifted and I felt quite rich.

Ezra painted a sign:

EZRA BEN-YICHYA
JEWELER & SILVERSMITH

and hung it outside our door. Through the front window passers-by could see him at work. Many stopped to watch him in fascination, and soon – hesitantly – a few people pushed open the door and came into his workshop.

Ezra had melted down the silver and mixed it with copper so that he could sell his jewelry more cheaply. He began by making tiny pendants in the shape of an open hand; this design is known as a *chamsah* and it is worn as a talisman by Jews of the Orient to ward off the Evil Eye.

Some Jewish women came into the shop to buy them, but we were puzzled when some Christian and Moslem women also purchased them.

"It is the hand of Mary," one Christian woman explained. Ezra just smiled. The Moslem customer said, "No, it is the hand of Fatima – the favorite daughter of the prophet Mohammed." I wanted to contradict them both, but a frown from Ezra signaled me to be still. After all, we had to eat, and if they saw in our jewelry something relevant to their lives, we would be foolish to discourage them.

Ezra worked long hours and I really had little to do, although the child within me was growing and I had become heavy and awkward. I prepared the savory meals that Ezra and I both enjoyed, spicing the meat and vegetables with cardamom, coriander, *chilbe* and *chawaij*. I baked *jachnun* – bread made from rolled dough, and sometimes I prepared *f'tut,* which I cut in small pieces and mixed with meat soup when we had enough money for a small piece of beef or a chicken.

When I couldn't think of anything else to do, I would sit in Ezra's front room and watch him work. He would sit on a woven mat, shaping sheet metal into a round form and I would see his clever hands deftly create a design in deep bas-relief by a process he called repousse'. He hammered, punched and shaped the metal from the back with special tools and I never tired of watching as the lovely designs emerged on the front surface.

"Everything you create is so beautiful, Ezra."

"Your father was a good teacher," he answered modestly.

"Would you...would you let me try?" I was embarrassed to ask, for this was not woman's work.

He laughed. "How many things do you want to learn? You are picking up new languages, from Sarah and the other women in the Rova. You are growing your herbs. And soon you will have a baby to tend."

It was true. I wanted to learn everything. I had started to speak both Yiddish and Hebrew, although with my Yemenite accent the women sometimes laughed at me. I could read, though Yifat and Sarah were the only ones who had discovered my secret. But the jewelry fascinated me.

"Here," Ezra said good-naturedly. "Try for yourself."

I did try, but my hands were awkward. My fingers felt thick, like plantains. "I can't do it!" I admitted, my eyes full of tears.

"Of course not, Mazal. It takes years to learn." Seeing my distress, he added: "If it means so much to you, you can help me sometimes – I will teach you."

"Like an apprentice?" I asked joyfully.

"No – like a wife who has too much time on her hands!" he joked. "Just for fun."

I nodded gratefully. And it was then that a sharp pain ripped through me, as though my back were caught in a metal vise. I bit my lip to stop from crying out. Ezra looked at me with concern. "What is it?"

The pain passed, so I just shook my head. He went

on with his work until a few minutes later I let out a scream.

"The baby?" he asked tremulously.

I remembered helping my mother when my little brothers and sisters were born. I nodded, longing for her now.

"I must take you to the hospital!" he cried. "I do not know what to do."

"No!" I implored him. "The hospitals are run by missionaries – they might steal our baby or try to convert me!"

"Who told you this?"

"Sarah. Please – do not take me there."

He suddenly looked the frightened nineteen-year-old boy that he was. "But I cannot deliver the baby myself!"

"Fetch Sarah. And Yifat," I screamed wildly. "They will take care of me."

"Are you sure?"

"Hurry – hurry!" I shouted.

Ezra flew out the door and I clung to the edge of his bench, bracing myself for the next pain.

Helping my mother and giving birth myself were two very different experiences, I discovered. Perhaps my mother had been braver or perhaps, after several children, it became easier, but with each pain I was sure I would die. It seemed an eternity before Ezra returned with Sarah and Yifat. Sarah did not even stop to reassure me; briskly she set about doing what was needed, and barked orders at Ezra to boil pots of water and bring clean cloths. Even in a delirium of pain, I was amazed: Would a man take orders from a woman? But after a startled glance, Ezra did as he was told while Sarah and Yifat tended me in the bedroom.

Yifat held my hand, her eyes filled with sympathy. "Oh, I remember how bad it was. It was terrible."

Sarah turned on her. "You are a silly, foolish girl and you are frightening her even more."

"Am I going to die?" I cried.

"Of course not. I've had seven babies and did I die from it? Well, neither will you."

At that moment our baby was born. With the first cry, Ezra's head again appeared around the door, "My son?" he asked.

Sarah smiled at him. "Your daughter. *Mazal tov!*"

6

WE NAMED OUR BABY
RUCHAMA, because Ezra said that
Hashem had been merciful with us. It was
true. We had made the journey from Yemen
without mishap and we had found a modest dwelling
with enough space for Ezra's workshop. Now he made
jewelry only from inexpensive materials – silver mixed
with copper, and glass instead of precious stones, but there
was a steady trickle of customers and, *Baruch Hashem,*
we always had enough to eat.

We were fortunate to have our little house. True, the
Ashpot Gate itself was not very aesthetically attractive,
as it was unadorned and hardly wide enough for a mule
cart to pass through, and, worse yet, it was the exit for
the city's trash. But the little house was ours. My friend
Yifat and her family lived in *Battei Machaseh*, the charity
shelters. They had been allocated rooms there until
Reuven found employment.

There were scores of families in Battei Machaseh,
all newcomers, who had been given these temporary
homes. They were not asked to pay rent – Jews in the
Golah supported them and they were allowed to stay for
three years, provided the menfolk devoted a specified
number of hours to study of the sacred texts. The Heavenly
reward for fulfilling the mitzvah of Torah study would
be credited to the benefactors as well. The recipients of
this charity were also required to observe what Sarah
called the *Yahrtzeit* – the anniversary of the death – of
their sponsors' relatives. Yifat was content there because

many of our Yemenite friends who had made the pilgrimage with us were among her neighbors.

The Battei Machaseh were in the most spacious part of the Rova. They consisted of a monumental structure bordering on the Deutscher Platz, German Square, the facade of which was a series of arches, crowned by the seal of the Baron Edmond de Rothschild – the rich Jew we knew of back in Sana'a as "Rashil." Because there was no space to socialize inside the houses, Yifat would take Evyatar into the Square to play and meet with all her neighbors. Sometimes I would take Ruchama over there too, carrying her in a sling I had fashioned from a length of cloth, and Yifat would laughingly talk about making a *shidduch* between our children when they came of age.

The place I really liked to visit was Sarah's home, and it was my dream that when we became rich – and I was sure that one day we would – we could buy a home there too. Sarah lived in the Chosh, on the west of the northern end of Chabad Street. "Chosh" is Arabic for a residential courtyard and this one was wonderfully picturesque. It was a veritable maze of dwellings, with curved stone staircases disappearing around corners and emerging again on the rooftop. From Sarah's roof I could see all the way across the Rova to the dome of the Churvah Synagogue. Twenty years earlier, this magnificent structure had been built on the ruins of one started by Rabbi Yehudah He-Chasid.

What I most loved about the Chosh courtyard was the garden. Two trees grew there laden with fruit or bursting with fragrant blossoms – an orange tree and a lemon tree. The oranges were wonderfully sweet and Sarah always gave me some to take home. She told me that few citrus trees flourished in the hilly climate of Jerusalem, but these, sheltered as they were in the courtyard, had been thriving for years. At the base of the trees, plants grew in wild profusion – many herbs all interspersed with yellow honeysuckle and scarlet anemones. It was not like my mother's wild herb garden, or even my tidy one, but I enjoyed the riot of color and the perfume of flowers against a backdrop of aging stone walls.

The courtyard was not the only attraction. I truly loved Sarah. Ezra found her pushy and domineering, being unaccustomed to the manner of Ashkenazi women. But he never forbade me to visit her, which would have broken my heart.

Sarah was a bustling, big-boned woman, invariably dressed in a floral print dress covered by a voluminous apron. She made her own clothes and although the materials might vary, the style was always the same: her dress buttoned down the front, had a neat high collar, long sleeves and a skirt wide enough for her to work in comfortably. Summer and winter, she wore heavy black boots and a dark turban that covered her hair, making her look quite forbidding. But when she smiled, her high cheek bones and bright eyes reminded me of Imma.

I soon learned that Sarah, despite the no-nonsense facade, was one of the kindest women ever created. She had seven children and one of them Naomi, was my age but still at school. "When will she marry?" I asked her, but Sarah just laughed. "Plenty of time," she would say. "She's only a child."

I found this very strange. I couldn't remember any girls of fifteen in Sana'a being unmarried, except for Dinah who was very plain and no one wanted to marry. But Sarah didn't seem the least concerned that her daughter should have reached such an age without a husband. She certainly wasn't ashamed of the fact as our Yemenite women would have been.

Sarah treated me like an extra daughter, but with a certain deference for my marital status. She sensed how much I missed my mother, and she tried to guide me in domestic matters. She told me which tradesmen were honest, showed me where I could buy the tenderest chickens and instructed me in the ways of the Rova. She baked wonderful bread and cakes and often sent me delicious braided *challot* before Shabbat, still warm from the oven. I tried to return the kindness by bringing her portions of meals I made, but although she always expressed gratitude, I sensed that my food was too highly spiced for her palate. What she did enjoy though, was my *gisher;* whenever she visited, she would drink cups and cups of it, and this gave me great pleasure.

I was starting to enjoy my life in Jerusalem. Having a baby to cuddle took away much of my loneliness and I made new friends in the community every day. Ruchama was really responsible for this: everyone loves a baby, and she, with her dark skin, glossy black curls, big brown eyes and happy nature, was a magnet that drew the girls and women of the Rova to us, asking permission to pick her up and hold her, and exclaiming over her exotic beauty.

Although new Jewish neighborhoods were starting to spring up outside the gates, I rarely ventured beyond the walls of the Old City. For me, the city was fixed and limited by the ancient walls, which had served the residents well for over three centuries. It was a big enough area for me, always teeming with people from dozens of different ethnic backgrounds. Sarah told me that when Suleiman the Magnificent had built the walls, he had intended to encircle Mount Zion as well, but somehow his engineers neglected to carry out this instruction. They were hanged for the oversight; and buried at the entrance to the city.

Often I accompanied Ezra to the *Kotel* early in the morning, before the shop was open, and it was from these visits that I had gotten the idea of embroidering the picture for my home. Gradually I had overcome my fear of the *Kotel,* but I was always awed by its majesty and sense of history, especially when I learned how old were the rows of stones – from the era of King Herod, then four rows from the Roman period, with smaller stones from the time of the Mamelukes and the Turks. Recently Montefiore had added courses at the top of the Wall to function as a barrier separating the Temple Mount compound from the Western Wall. This largely prevented the Arabs, who had built a mosque on the site of our Holy Temple, from throwing stones and garbage on the Jews praying below.

Ezra had told me on our first visit that the Divine Presence never abandons the Western Wall, a thought which initially had frightened me. There was only a small area for prayer, about twenty-eight meters long and four meters wide. Surrounding it were the ramshackle dwellings of immigrants from North Africa, huddled in a wretched clutter of slums.

To reach the *Kotel*, we had to wind our way through filthy, twisting alleyways so dark and gloomy that we could not see anything until we emerged right at the foot of the Wall. The Arabs hated our going there to pray, and the Turks forbade us even to light candles there or set up chairs for the elderly to pray more comfortably. The Moslems named it "el Burak," after their prophet Mohammed's horse, and claimed that the beast had ascended to heaven from there so that they also could lay claim to it.

Nevertheless, Ezra went there every morning in the

pearly dawn, and in fine weather I would often go too, with Ruchama in her sling and bundled up under the warm shawl I had woven for her. I did not know any formal prayers by heart, and I did not want Ezra to see me reading from a Siddur (Sarah was helping me to learn but I still felt ashamed of my new skill), so I would stand off to the side and make up my own prayers.

If there was room, I would actually touch and kiss the stones and a strange energy seemed to flow into me. I prayed for my husband's work to be successful; I prayed that my baby should stay healthy; I prayed for my friends; and of course I prayed that one day my father and mother and brothers and sisters could join us in Jerusalem. Then I would wait for Ezra, as I was petrified to walk back alone lest I would meet any Arabs who were setting out for work. There were stories of what they might do to Jewish women.

When we got home, I would make breakfast and tend the baby while Ezra hurried off to the *beit midrash* to learn the Talmud with a group of scholars who had made his acquaintance. They had approached him one day at the *Kotel,* when they noticed how fervently he prayed and the devotion with which he donned his *tefillin,* to invite him to join their *shiur.* It was their intention to complete the cycle of learning the entire Talmud in seven years.

Ezra was honored to have been asked to participate. Often, when he returned from the *beit midrash* his face was aglow and I could hear him softly repeating to himself the passages he'd studied, as he braced the front door of the shop wide open and settled down to work. He had amassed a substantial stock of trinkets in these past months and although they could not compare with the elegant gold jewelry he had made in Sana'a, people would come to admire them and occasionally buy something for a special occasion.

Ezra kept his word about teaching me his craft. Whenever he wasn't busy, he would let me try my hand at the different techniques. I showed some skill at piercing – stamping out small areas from the metal with a sharp, chisel-like tool. I also could manage granulation, taking tiny beads or chips of metal and fusing them to create a raised pattern.

My efforts were far too amateurish to sell, but I loved to make little gifts for my friends, like the dangling earrings for Yifat that glittered with fragments of blue glass, or the brooch I made for Sarah, with a cluster of five granules in the center to represent the five books of the Torah. She told me she would treasure it forever and she has loyally worn it pinned to her collar ever since. Although it was not a terribly expensive piece, and the workmanship was inferior, I believe it is the most valuable thing she owns!

Sarah constantly urged me to learn new things and always encouraged me when I was unsure.

"Have you told Ezra that you can read?" she would challenge me.

I would lower my eyes. "It is not seemly for a woman."

"Nonsense. That is the Arab mentality. Hashem gave men and women wisdom and understanding – and you mustn't let your abilities go to waste. Ezra should be proud of you."

But I knew it would trouble him, so I kept it a secret. I sensed he was afraid that I would forget our Yemenite traditions and the respect women always showed for their husbands. In spite of this, he was far more tolerant than most Yemenite men. After all, he did indulge me about letting me try silversmithing, and I felt he was actually proud of my ability to pick up languages because it was helpful with customers, although he never remarked on it. But there was still a *gevul,* an invisible border, that I did not wish to cross. I knew that one day my Ruchama would go to school and learn to read and write and she would cross many more borders than I ever dreamed of, and this was enough for me.

Every Friday morning I would paint the outside of our house bright blue, as high as I could reach. One day Sarah came past on her way from the market and surprised me at my task.

"What on earth are you doing?" she asked.

"It's to keep away the evil spirits," I told her. "I do it every week, and so far, it has been effective."

"Good heavens, girl. You're not serious!"

I nodded. "We always have done so. My mother too. Do you not have this tradition?"

My friend smiled and her voice softened. "How do you think it keeps them away?"

"Well, when they come to get us, they see the blue color and they become confused. They think it's the sky, so they go away."

"I didn't mean to ridicule you," she said apologetically. "If that is your tradition, I suppose it's all right." She kissed me on the cheek. I knew she thought I was foolish, but my mother had done it and her mother before her, and even here in Jerusalem, I saw that quite a few of my neighbors did the same thing. Sarah knew many things, but she didn't know everything. And I was taking no chances on an evil spirit coming to snatch my baby, my husband or me.

Ezra came out of his workroom. "What did Sarah want?" he asked curiously.

I shrugged. "She was just passing by."

He looked approvingly at my work. "It is good," he commented, "but you missed a spot – over there."

7

I WAS BEGINNING TO UNDERSTAND how so many psalms and songs had been written in praise of the beauty of Jerusalem. I can't imagine how I ever thought of it as dark and forbidding.

The city seemed to nestle comfortably among the Judean hills, almost like a natural outcropping in the mountainous terrain. Its very stones were imbued with millennia of history and it had a jewel-like glow that was golden in sunshine and silver in moonlight, just as Ezra had once described it to me.

Sarah had become my mentor, and from her I was learning the history of Jerusalem and its people – an ever-changing tapestry of those who had been drawn to the city from the four corners of the earth.

Sarah was the daughter of a leader of the Chasidic community, Nisan Bak; in fact, the largest Chasidic synagogue in the Rova, Tiferet Yisrael, was popularly known as the Nisan Bak Synagogue. It had been completed fifteen years before our arrival, and it was named in honor of Rav Yisrael of Ruzhin, Sarah's grandfather.

Her own father, Nisan Bak, was still alive, although quite old, and lived in her house. She told me that her family, in addition to being great Talmudic scholars, had been printers for many generations and at one time had published a Hebrew newspaper called *Chavatzelet*. Sarah's father, Rabbi Yisrael's son, was born in Berdichev in the Ukraine and came to Palestine with his father in

1831. The old printing press was sold recently, but her home was filled with volumes of books printed by her family, which she would show me very proudly. There was the *Midrash Tanchuma* printed by Jacob Bak centuries earlier, and a magnificent set of *machzorim* printed by Jacob and Joseph Bak that was dated 1680. In elegant micrography, the frame on the title page specified festivals for which the prayer book was designed. The printer's mark of her grandfather and her father was a woodcut of Jerusalem which depicted the Western Wall, the Temple Mount and the Mount of Olives.

After her father sold the printing press, he devoted himself exclusively to the community in the Rova. He was very active among the Chasidim and was the representative of the Ruzhin-Sadigora dynasty in Jerusalem. It was through his contacts with the Turkish Government, who respected his authority and his court, that many decrees against the Jews were modified. Ezra's objections to my spending so much time with Sarah were lessened when he learned that apart from building the Tiferet Yisrael synagogue, Nisan Bak was also the founder of the new Ezrat Niddachim Society which was combatting the missionaries and was helping to establish a Yemenite quarter in Jerusalem. The missionaries were an ever-present threat to the Rova's poor Jews, trying to win over souls with bribes of food, medicines and money, and in some cases they succeeded.

Sarah's husband, Efrayim Fishl Levy, was a great scholar and *Rosh Yeshivah*. He was a member of the Rivlin family – apparently a genuine distinction, as the family had lived in Jerusalem for seven generations.

Spring had come to Jerusalem and the air was soft and warm. Sometimes, we would discover a wildflower that had forced its way through a crevice in the stones – a red poppy or a creamy pink cyclamen looking delicate but with a will strong enough to survive in such inhospitable soil. "Like our people," I would think to myself. Ruchama was toddling now and she would try to uproot the flower in her little dimpled fist until I gently restrained her. Ezra doted on her and would let her play with his baskets of beads to her heart's content. She was to have a brother or sister just after her second birthday.

I was feeling much better than in my first pregnancy. Letters came from my father passing on messages from Imma that I should drink lots of melissa tea, which Sarah called lemon balm. She would have pulled it out of her garden, thinking it was a weed, but I knew it had wonderful properties. Sarah taught me so much; it gave me a lot of satisfaction to be able to tell her some things that she didn't know.

"You infuse the leaves in boiling water and the tea makes you feel calm," I told her. "It will give you long life."

"Are you sure it won't poison me?" she asked doubtfully.

I laughed. "If that were so, we would all be dead long ago. Imma says that melissa tea is also good for earache and toothache, and it stops the stomach sickness when the woman is with child. The leaves have a lovely lemony scent – you can stuff them into a small pillow to make the room smell fresh."

Gradually I allayed her suspicions and she told me she had started to make melissa tea as an evening drink for herself and her husband and father. They all declared it was indeed relaxing and helped them to sleep better.

With the spring had come preparations for Pesach. The year before, on our first Pesach in Yerushalayim, Ezra had wanted everything to be the same as in Sana'a, but it had not been possible. I had done my best, but I knew Ezra had been disappointed, although he had not uttered one word of criticism. This year I was determined to please him. Our Yemenite traditions were very important to him. It did not seem to matter to Ezra that things were done differently here.

In Yemen all the wheat for the matzot was supervised from the time it was harvested, and then it was carried home in special sacks and spread out on white sheets where each grain was carefully inspected and sorted. I remembered how my father would wash and scrape the grinding stone before grinding the wheat.

Then my mother kept the flour in a special ceramic jug until the eve of Passover, when a team of three women would bake the first matzot for their families together. Even the water they used was carefully stored after being drawn from a well in a special vessel at night. My mother would mix the dough, her sister would pour the water, and my father's sister would tend the fire and bake. The women in Sana'a made a fresh batch of matzot every morning of *Chol Ha-moed* – the between-days of the Festival. They arose at dawn to knead the dough and gather wood for the ovens. By breakfast time, the freshly-baked matzot were on the table.

For some reason, here in Eretz Yisrael the *men* did all the matza-baking! With their lack of experience in food preparation, it was little wonder that their matzot were so flavorless. But the care that they took in guarding the wheat and the water and so forth was as meticulous as ours ever was. In that regard, at least, Ezra had been satisfied.

This year, I wanted to make *charoset* for the Seder like we'd had at home, although it was complicated. There we had ground all the ingredients in a copper mortar – every Yemenite had one, but I had forgotten to bring it with me. Our *charoset* had such an exotic aroma and taste: ground dates, raisins, nuts, sesame and pomegranate seeds were mixed with wine and honey. Some of these ingredients were expensive and hard to come by, but I scoured the shuk and bargained fiercely with the shopkeepers until I had them all at a price we could afford.

This small victory gave me confidence. I knew now that I *could* make our Jerusalem Pesach like my parents' *chag*. Last year's Ashkenazi *charoset,* kindly provided by Sarah, had been as bland as her chicken soup was!

In Sana'a, our home was made of mud and always before Pesach we had plastered and whitewashed the walls. It was also the Yemenite custom to buy or make new clothes for Passover. Even poor families were given money for this purpose from a special communal fund. Some charitable women sewed dresses for those in need, and wealthy families donated clothes anonymously. They would leave them at the door late at night and it was my hope that one day, if I were rich enough, I could do this also, even in Jerusalem.

We had been invited to the Bak-Levy home for the Seder, but we politely refused, explaining that our Seder would be according to Yemenite tradition. We held it together with Yifat and Reuven and the children – Evyatar now had two adorable little sisters. The men sat on the floor around a low table, leaning on big pillows, and each of them had his own Seder plate. I had decked the table with greenery: leaves of parsley, radishes, green onions, lettuce and celery.

While Yifat and I served and cleared away and brought them water for washing, Ezra and Reuven recited the Haggadah together. At one point I forgot myself and joined in. Six pairs of eyes looked at me in astonishment. It was not our custom for women to participate in the singing, let alone the recitation.

"How do you know the words?" Reuven asked me in amazement. "You can't read, can you?"

I blushed. "I remember the words from my father's Seder," I told him.

Ezra regarded me uncomfortably – I think he had guessed my secret, but he said nothing. After that, I concentrated on my chores and thanked the Almighty in my heart. The Children of Israel were freed from Egyptian bondage and we were relatively free in the Holy City of Yerushalayim, despite the occasionally harsh Ottoman rule.

There were certain legends in Aramaic that children in Yemen were trained to recite, but Ruchama and Evyatar were still too young. We gave them nuts and raisins to keep them awake. In Sana'a the longing for Jerusalem had been the central theme of the Seder and I remembered how my father always cried as he drank the first cup of wine representing the Exile, hoping for an early Redemption. He would leave the door open for the whole of Pesach just in case Mashiach would come.

The next morning the pains started two weeks early. Perhaps it was due to all my extra physical exertions for the Passover preparations. I was relieved, though, to know that there would only be one Seder night; in Yemen, we had always had two, but in Eretz Yisrael there was just the one. Having my baby would not interfere with my holiday duties.

Once again, Ezra raced to get Yifat and Sarah to help me. This time, however, all my help came from Above, for by the time they breathlessly arrived, our beautiful baby son had also made his appearance. All Sarah had to do was cut the cord. In truth, it had been a great deal less painful than before. And this time, I had plastered the outside of our home blue before Pesach, so I knew that the evil spirits would not come in to harm me or my baby.

"I am so proud of you," Sarah said warmly. I smiled to myself. It would not have been seemly for me to act like a child. After all, I was now a mature woman – I was already seventeen years old.

8

THEY SAY THAT
DISASTER casts long shadows, but I
was never filled with a sense of foreboding
that my contented life might change. From the
time of Ruchama's birth, and then Assaf's, the future
looked bright. Ezra, with his clever hands, was making a
good living and people talked of the beauty of his craft.
Some officials from Constantinople began dropping in
to the workshop to buy trinkets. They had plenty of money
and they desired the best, so once again Ezra began to
work with gold, silver and precious jewels. Some of the
Turks ordered decorations for their saddles and bridles,
holders for playing cards (they loved to gamble), rings
and snuff boxes and belt buckles. These items all bore
our traditional Yemenite designs of plaited silver and gold,
and even the *Magen David* or pomegranate was often
part of the pattern, but it didn't seem to worry the
customers. Perhaps they were unaware of the Jewish
significance and simply found the designs attractive.

Many scholars had settled in Jerusalem in the last
150 years, and now many more were following in their
footsteps. This delighted Ezra, who had finally managed
to overcome his distrust of Ashkenazi Jews. One of the
very first to return had been Rav Avraham Gershon of
Kutow, brother-in-law of the Baal Shem Tov, who arrived
a few years after the Arabs had broken into the Ashkenazi
synagogue and burnt the precious Scrolls. Dozens of
students of Rabbi Eliyahu, the Vilna Gaon, had brought
their families here from Lithuania, and their descendants

– including Efrayim Fishl's family – formed the core of the *Yishuv.* Sephardim had also come, like Rav Chaim ben Moshe Attar of Sale', who came to the Holy City with his disciples from Italy and established a big yeshivah. The recent arrivals were by no means coming to a Torah wasteland – they could have their pick of academies and houses of worship. As Sarah explained to me: "Competition among scholars increases wisdom," and indeed Jerusalem was becoming a great center of wisdom and learning.

The "melting-pot" atmosphere in Jerusalem had changed Ezra, to my surprise and great pleasure. The Yemenite traditions were still very important to him, but gradually he realized that there was no need to be ashamed if people knew that his wife could read. He was now quite willing for me to be in the shop and speak to customers because, we discovered, I had a natural facility for languages. Ezra spoke Arabic and Aramaic and Hebrew; English, French and Yiddish were quite beyond him, though I had picked them up with relative ease. He was even grateful for my help.

I was also becoming more skillful with the jewelry and some of my efforts he had deemed good enough to display. We now had three beautiful children: Shalom had joined Ruchama and Assaf, all born in the Holy Land. One day I came home from the market with the three children and I could see that Ezra had something exciting to tell me. His eyes were shining and a smile hovered around his lips.

"You have some good news?" I asked.

"Feed the children and put them down for their nap, and then I will tell you."

I knew better than to press him to tell me before he was ready, so I did as he bade me, full of curiosity The two boys were plump and placid and gave me no trouble. Ruchama, however, was interested in neither food nor sleep. At six, she was a dreamer, a lover of beauty. She enjoyed drawing pictures and would stand in my garden admiring the herbs and flowers for hours on end. She also loved watching her father create jewelry. Her tiny hands, with their long, sensitive fingers, would hover over the baskets and often Ezra would let her choose the jewel to be set. Finally, when the three children were asleep, I went into the workshop.

"The necklace you made with the silver bells? It was sold today!"

I gasped. "Who bought it?"

"A Turk. He wanted a gift for his daughter and he liked your necklace. Here – this is for you."

He pressed some money into my hand. "Ezra! So much!"

"Buy yourself a present, Mazal. You earned it."

"Perhaps I'll buy the children new shoes..."

"No, you always buy for the children. This money is just for you. You are becoming a clever artisan."

I was touched. "I will never be like you, Ezra. I will never be able to create beauty like this." My hands went automatically to the pomegranate pendant which I had worn every day since our marriage seven years earlier.

"For a woman, you do very good work," my husband assured me. Compliments did not come easily to Ezra, so I knew I had pleased him very much. I felt proud of the partnership we had built. When we were married, we were almost strangers, but now we had not only founded a family, we were working together quite openly. In Sana'a it could never have happened. I was suffused with love for my husband who had elevated me to a status undreamed of for a woman in Yemen.

Ezra had many dealings with the Turkish Moslem administrators in Jerusalem, and always found that they dealt fairly with the Jews and Christians. Because we too believed in one God, they regarded us as protected peoples, but we were still forbidden to do many things. We could not ride horses or carry weapons. We paid higher taxes than the Moslems. But Ezra still maintained that we would be treated fairly if we observed the law. European consulates and many religious institutions had been set up in Jerusalem, so it was no longer practical for the Turks to discriminate against the Jewish and Christian population.

There was a Moslem religious court which had the power to judge on all aspects of the law. A Turkish judge was assisted by four Arab deputy judges, who often took bribes. Many times judgments were influenced by cash payments, but it didn't seem to matter what the donor's faith was: if he paid enough, he would get the favorable judgment. We were lucky in Jerusalem that the Moslem punishment practiced in Yemen – amputating limbs for crimes such as theft – was never imposed, but there were fines, whippings and prison sentences.

Still, we were law-abiding citizens as were our friends, and life was not too severe. My only sorrow was that my family was still in Sana'a. The two Moslem apprentices whom my father had been ordered to train as silversmiths were lacking in any kind of artistic skill and their progress was so slow as to be nonexistent. Perhaps we had inherited the artistry from the Biblical Betzalel for my father and Ezra executed work of great beauty and delicacy. And apparently I was learning too: I could make fine silver filigree that looked like lace and had progressed to granulation. Some of my happiest hours were spent working side-by-side with my husband, after the children had gone to sleep.

When he sang *Eshet Chayil* – "Woman of Valor" – on Friday nights, I knew he was well-pleased with me. I think he really believed that my worth was above rubies. Our life together was very harmonious and tranquil. Our children were our fulfillment: solemn Ruchama, the dreamer; Assaf, clever and full of mischief; and fat, happy baby Shalom, gurgling with pleasure at the antics of his brother. People pointed us out as a special family, and from a shy, hesitant girl I now felt confident and accomplished. Ezra had also been just a boy when we arrived, but now he was well-respected in the community and not only by the Jews, who appreciated his pious ways and scholarship; his Moslem customers would ask his advice and opinion on many different matters. I was so terribly proud of him.

In many ways, we were two completely different people from the young couple who had arrived in the Holy Land seven years earlier. Ezra had been barely nineteen years old, yet he bolstered my courage. Although in his heart he was really unsure of himself that he could carry off the role of husband, father and provider – until then, he had worked only under my father's direction – he had displayed a manliness and sense of responsibility well beyond his years.

And I – what had I been? A semi-literate child who had been without any cares, suddenly plunged into a new life with not nearly enough preparation for it. Yet here I was: a wife, a mother, a budding jeweler, a linguist – and even an herbalist, for once when I cured a neighbor of a fever, she had told others and now they often came to the shop to consult me.

"The pride of man will bring him low," we are told. Perhaps I did need a lesson in humility, but not very far in the future loomed a lesson that was almost too painful to bear, that would alter our happy family life forever.

9

IT IS WRITTEN: "Jerusalem, which is bound firmly together, binds the Jews one to the other." This was the way our life was. We were kind to each other in those days and truly helped one another. Ezra's business continued to prosper, and I was able to assist neighbors who were less fortunate than we were – my dream come true. Often, as evening shadows lengthened, I would slip out of the house and leave a basket of food on the doorstep of someone who I knew could not afford to feed his hungry family. Young as they were, I wanted to teach my children the same lessons of charity and good deeds that my parents had taught me. Ruchama was seven, Assaf was five, and Shalom only three, but I still felt a great responsibility to do this, as well as to tell them about their Yemenite traditions.

I would gather them around me and show them an old sepia photograph, now cracked and wrinkled, but which I still treasured: my parents.

"This is Djeddi and this is Djedda," I would explain.

The two boys would nod solemnly, but Ruchama always had questions. "Are those their names?"

"Here we would say *Saba* and *Savta* – grandfather and grandmother," I would tell her, "but I want you to keep the old names from Sana'a. It would please them."

"When will they come to Jerusalem?" Shalom would ask. "Will they bring me a present?"

"It would be the biggest present just to have them here," I would chide him. "Djedda is a wonderful lady.

Whatever she has, she shares with her neighbors – food, medicines, even clothes. And no one knows who brings them the things they need. She keeps it a secret."

"Then how can they say 'thank you'?" baby Shalom would ask, mindful of the good manners his father always stressed.

"She doesn't need thanks. She gets her reward just knowing she has helped someone."

Then I would describe the Jewish Quarter where we had lived in Sana'a and where their grandparents still lived. We had not been forced to live there by the Moslem masters, but rather we had built the wall to keep them out and to maintain our identity and culture untainted by foreign influences. However, when we left for Eretz Yisrael, it was that very protective enclosure that made our houses unsellable: no Moslem wanted to live there. That was of no interest to the children, of course, and, praise God, no longer very important. They savored the stories of the old country, and I savored the retelling.

It made me very happy just to know that Jerusalem was our home now. It *was* a beautiful city, especially when seen from on high. I would often climb to the roof of the Chosh where Sarah lived to see the area around the Temple Mount. I would imagine the crowds of pilgrims gathering there at the three Festivals to bring sacrifices in the Holy Temple. There was a vast panorama of domed roofs and towers, dusty alleys and broad boulevards. Looking no bigger than ants, people shopped and strolled and went to pray at the *Kotel.* When viewed from such a height, the city's walls and gates and ramparts formed all kinds of fascinating patterns.

The roofs of the Rova were knobby white domes, while the Christian Quarter favored red-tiled roofs. Twisting alleys wound maze-like through the city. These were the very streets where the great men and women of the Torah had strode, and I felt so privileged that we were following in the footsteps of David and Solomon. Yet Jerusalem, city of peace, throughout the centuries had been the site of savage fighting, death and destruction.

Death still stalked its streets. Most of the streets and the houses were badly drained. Stagnant water was a breeding ground for mosquitos and flies, and rainwater collected in cisterns which sometimes were polluted by sewage. Sickness was an ever-present visitor to our neighborhood. I was grateful that my mother had taught me so much about remedies and had given me such a good example to follow. I kept our little house scrupulously clean and never allowed the children to touch any foul thing they found on the street; that is what Imma had done. I knew no other way.

At the first sign of illness, my instinct was to make the children a *ptisan* of the flowers and leaves of the chamomile plant I grew. Its blue oil healed many things: it aided digestion after a heavy meal, soothed pain, and was a disinfectant. It flowered half of the year, from May until October – lovely fragrant blossoms with a yellow hollow and conical receptacle for the pollen. I would dry the flowers and make tea from them and I always had a ready supply in big glass jars.

That was why I didn't worry too much when Ezra began to complain of a fever and listlessness. I made him tall glasses of my chamomile tea and urged him to rest. The children's noise worried him, which was unusual because he loved to play with them. I sent them to their friends' homes during the day and I worked in the shop, continuously bustling in and out of Ezra's room with my healing teas and nourishing food.

Nothing seemed to help. His nose bled and his skin

erupted with small oval pink spots on his chest and back. He was feverish and couldn't sleep. I sent the children to stay at Sarah's.

"You must take him to the hospital!" she insisted.

But I was stubborn. "I will treat him myself," I cried angrily. I was still afraid of the missionaries and believed that they would cure my husband's body but steal his soul. "I will make him better."

"Mazal" she said quietly, "from what you tell me, Ezra is very sick. I think he has typhoid."

"No!" I screamed. "I will cure him!"

"Take him to the hospital!"

"Tomorrow," I said wildly. "If he is not better tomorrow."

All night I sat at his bedside, sponging his feverish brow and tending him when he became too weak to go to the outhouse. I was frantic with worry and decided that at first light, despite my fears, I would order a horsecart and take him to the hospital.

Towards morning, Ezra called out my name. "I am right here, my husband." He spoke through cracked, parched lips and the words came out in a whisper. "Mazal, you'll take good care of the children?"

"What do you mean? We'll take care of them together. As soon as you're better, they'll come home."

He seemed not to hear me. "Ruchama is very clever, very artistic. But she is frail not strong like her brothers."

"Why must we talk of this now? You must rest, my husband."

"No time," he whispered. "Assaf is a good scholar. He should learn – at a great yeshivah. He has the head for it. Don't worry too much about a trade for him unless you need the money."

I started to cry, but he went on. "Shalom will be difficult..."

"But he's just a baby!"

"You will have problems. He is headstrong. Already I see it. Watch over him...

He closed his eyes. I clutched his hands in mine and my tears fell on them unnoticed. "I love you," I sobbed, but there was no answer. Just as the first rays of light delicately brushed Jerusalem's grey stones, dappling them with gold, Ezra's soul slipped away to return to its Maker.

Outside, the city was bathed in sunlight, but on this day – and for many long days to come – the world for me was only darkness.

10

THE FIRST WEEKS after Ezra died passed in a blur of misery. During the week of *shivah,* it seemed that everyone in the Jewish Quarter came to console me. There was an endless procession of faces, but apart from Yifat and Sarah, there were none I really wanted to be with. If people brought food, I ate, but the food – like my life – had lost its flavor.

"Mazal, you haven't asked me about the children," Sarah chided me one day.

I felt apathetic. "It's kind of you to look after them," I muttered.

"I'm sending them home!"

"Not yet!" I pleaded. "I haven't the strength – it's too soon."

"Nonsense. They have been with me for three weeks now. They've lost their father; must they lose their mother as well? Ruchama has bad dreams – she cries out in the night. And the two boys don't laugh anymore. You must think of them, Mazal."

I sighed deeply. "How will I support them? What will become of us?"

"Oh, for heaven's sake, pull yourself together and stop whining. Where is your faith in the Almighty? You are a young woman of twenty-two with lots of strength. How will you support them? Why, you'll keep Ezra's business going, that's how."

My eyes widened. "I?! A silversmith?"

"Why not? You've been helping him for years."

"But I'm a woman...

"Yes, I'd noticed." Sarah gave a short laugh. "This is not Yemen, Mazal. It is quite respectable for a woman to earn an honest livelihood in any way she can. Why should you clean houses or take in laundry when you have this talent? Ezra sold a lot of your jewelry and the customers like you."

I shook my head. "I'm not good enough. I haven't even learned dapping properly."

"What on earth is dapping?"

"Well you take some flat metal and place it in a concave shape and hammer it into a dome. Ezra would join two tiny domes that way to make a silver bead. Those beads are a central part of Yemenite design, and I can't seem to get it right."

"Do you have tools for this?"

"Oh, yes. Ezra brought his special dapping block from Sana'a and the round-tipped tool you use with a hammer."

"So you'll teach yourself. As my American cousin often says: 'Necessity is the mother of invention.' When you have to, you'll do it."

Sarah always sounded brusque, it was just her manner. If she had sat with me and lamented my fate, I would have been rendered more helpless. I wanted her to hold and comfort me like a mother, but she knew better: what I needed was her no-nonsense attitude and some practical solutions.

She brought the children home to me the next day. I was shocked at how they looked. Wallowing in my own misery, I had hardly given them a thought, but Ruchama was hollow-eyed and thin; Assaf, quiet and withdrawn; and Shalom, tearful and angry. They were too young to have to face such a traumatic loss – but so was I! And now I would have to be both mother and father to them, nurture them, raise them, educate them and support them. The prospect overwhelmed me and I sank into despair.

In a way, it was Yifat who helped me even more than Sarah. She came over one evening after the children were asleep. "Mazal," she said tentatively, "Reuven has a friend. From Sana'a..."

"So?"

She hesitated. "He is not handsome and not so young. But he has a little bit of money. He's a merchant. He can take care of you and the children."

"Why are you telling me this?"

"He has seen you in the shop. He admires you. Maybe you should meet him and..."

I stood up, flushed and angry. "Yifat, stop it! No one will replace Ezra, my beloved husband. I do not need a man to take care of me and to bring up my children. I can do it alone!"

In that moment of anger, a resolution was born in me and I felt a surge of maturity and responsibility. I could do it; I *would* do it!

Yifat was frightened by my angry tone. "How ever will you manage?"

I sighed. She was not to blame. In Yemen, it was inconceivable that a Jewish woman could earn a living, and in her own business, no less. It was not possible for her to raise children with no husband. It was the men who learned, disciplined and educated the children, made the decisions and usually also had some craft or other means of livelihood. Women stayed at home and tended to household chores.

I took Yifat's hand. "I didn't mean to shout at you. I know you are trying to help. But I don't want another husband."

Yifat shook her head, her eyes full of tears. "We are leaving the Old City, Mazal."

"Why?" I asked in dismay.

She placed a hand on her swollen form, pregnant with her fourth child. "We can't stay where we are any longer – we need more space. We've looked for a place to rent, but many of the houses in the Rova are owned by Arabs and our friends tell us that when they have to renew their leases each year, the landlords demand higher and higher rental fees."

I felt my face go pale. Surely Ezra had dealt with the rent? In my misery, I had completely forgotten that we had purchased the house, when it was nothing but a miserable hovel. No, I calmed myself, I needn't worry about paying the rent. "Where are you going to live?"

"With a group of other families from Yemen. We are going to Shiloach."

This village, just outside the Ashpot Gate, was known to the Arabs as Silwan. It was on a steep hill overlooking the Kidron Valley, by the Shiloach pool. I had heard that some of the poorest Jews were living there in caves.

"It is not too far, Yifat. I can walk there. We still will see each other."

She nodded. "They say there are bandits. I am afraid, but Reuven says we can have a little house with a garden and it is cheap. Shall we look for something for you too?"

I shook my head. "I must stay here, where there are customers. Many pilgrims are coming now – Jewish and Christian – and they often want gifts to take home." I drew myself up straight. "I have a business to run.

The news that my dear friend and many of my countrymen would be moving away further depressed me. Except for Sarah, there was now no one to turn to for advice and help. I still hoped my parents would be allowed to come to Jerusalem, but they were getting older, the Moslem apprentices were lazy and making little progress, and I also realized it would be foolish for them to come unless they could sell their house and belongings. There was already too much poverty in Jerusalem and I would not be able to help them. My brothers and sisters had already come but were working in agricultural settlements at Rishon l'Tziyon and I had only seen them once since their arrival.

Much building activity was taking place in Jerusalem. The population had grown to 40,000, of which 25,000 were Jews. But they were not doing all the rebuilding; Catholics and Protestants, Greeks and Moslems were all building their own institutions. It was said that more than 100 new buildings were going up in the new suburbs, all of carefully cut stone with iron girders to support the ceiling which was then covered in French tiles instead of the more picturesque domes we were used to. But despite the city spreading outside the walls, I felt more secure in the Jewish Quarter and believed this was the best place to continue running Ezra's workshop.

After Yifat left, I prepared to retire. I dressed for bed and looked in the mirror. It seemed impossible that the trauma I had undergone had not altered me beyond recognition, but my reflection showed little change. Even in my shapeless cotton robe, I could still see the young woman I had been. I brushed my hair and the long tresses, tucked under a headscarf during the day, fell past my shoulders, lustrous and black. I tried to look at my face dispassionately, remembering that Ezra had always told me that I was beautiful. My skin was very dark, but smooth and unlined. My cheekbones were high, like my mother's, my chin pointed and determined. Only my eyes seemed to have grown older – they were deep brown, fringed with long, dark lashes but the light in them had dimmed from the many days of tears. I straightened my shoulders and tried to smile but it was tremulous.

Before retiring, I went into the children's room. The boys were asleep, Assaf's bedclothes a tangled mess as though he'd been thrashing around on his pallet. I straightened the blankets and kissed both boys on the forehead. They didn't stir. Ruchama, however, was lying on her mat, her solemn eyes following my every move. I remembered Ezra's words: "She is frail" and I felt afraid for her.

"Are you all right, Ruchama?" I asked, sitting on the edge of her pallet and caressing her pale cheek.

"Will we never see Abba again?" she asked quietly.

"After the Mashiach comes, the dead will rise again," I told her, aware that it would be of little comfort to a seven-year-old.

"When will that be, Imma?"

I shrugged. "We don't know. But every day we await his coming."

"I will help you, Imma. Don't send us away again.

"Was Sarah not kind to you?" I asked in sudden panic.

"She is very kind and so are her children. But you are our mother – we need to be with you."

I felt ashamed. "You are right! I promise never send you away again."

Sleep did not come to me again that night. We had saved a little money and I had a stock of jewelry that Ezra had completed, enough to keep us for a month or two. I decided to spend a few days just with the children, helping them to cope with the unbearable loss we had all sustained, before reopening the workshop.

We went for walks together all over the Old City. Shalom never tired of patting the "garbage donkeys," the beasts of burden which had baskets slung over their backs to remove the city's refuse. Sometimes he fed them carrot tops and they would nuzzle his hands. Assaf had lost much of his mischievousness and, although only five, was almost paternal towards his little brother as if already preparing himself for the role of man of the family.

Ruchama, a lovely dark-haired child who liked me to dress her all in white – even her stockings – spoke little on our walks, but she saw everything and responded to each beautiful thing, whether a wildflower, a butterfly or a smooth pebble. "How pretty, Imma!" she would exclaim, stretching out delicate fingers towards the object. It was hard to know what she was thinking.

"Such a serious child," the neighbors would comment, as their own daughters played Five Stones or skipped rope in the narrow alleys. They thought she was unfriendly, but I understood. Ruchama was satisfied to be alone to commune with nature. She enjoyed solitude.

For me, solitude was a burden I would have to learn to live with. Many times during the day, my hands would move to my throat and instinctively seek the golden pomegranate on its chain encircling my neck. At least that was left to me as a tangible reminder of the gentle husband who had enriched my life in so many ways.

11

THE NECESSITY OF EARNING a living and tending the children forced me out of my apathy. "There is a time to mourn and a time to dance" – no, I did not feel like dancing, but the time for mourning had passed. By no means did the pain disappear; it simply became a part of me, like an extra limb or organ that was ever-present but could not consume all of my attention. I needed to maintain the shop and to take care of my appearance, for the sake of business; I had to talk to customers and greet them with a smile. I even laughed occasionally – particularly at things my little Shalom would say. "You've put your shoes on the wrong feet!" I scolded him one day. "But they're the only feet I've got," was his quick reply. His twinkling eyes confirmed that, little as he was, he knew he had made a good joke.

Customers seemed to throng to the shop. I would have thought that they came out of pity for the young widow, except for the fact that most of them were strangers and many were not even Jewish. Ten thousand Christian pilgrims made the journey to Jerusalem every year from places as distant as Portugal, Muscovy and Scandinavia. The stock of jewelry that Ezra had left was soon depleted and I realized I had to make a lot more without delay.

Fortunately, I knew where Ezra had always acquired his supplies of materials and how much he paid for them, as he'd left a neat pile of receipts. So, in between tending customers, I would work on new designs, continuing late into the night, after the children were asleep. It was not hard physical work and it filled the lonely hours. Some of my pieces were not successful at first, but I could always melt them down and rework them. I had had a good teacher – the best, in fact. He would have been proud of his student's accomplishments.

Another factor contributing to the success of my shop was the absence of competition. No other Jews had established such a business in the Old City and the Arabs, for religious reasons, did not engage in it. Their Moslem bible, the Koran, held that gold and precious stones in this life were corrupting, so the Arabs had no ambition to make the items themselves. They believed that jewelry was one of the rewards of the Moslem paradise, not to be indulged here on earth. They were also not in favor of women displaying a lot of jewelry and thought it better reserved for the houris of paradise. That was why the Jews had been the goldsmiths in Yemen and it was only after so many artisans like my Ezra had left, that the Arabs realized they must also train their own people in the craft or they would be entirely bereft of adornment. Paradoxically, despite the mild prohibition in their sacred texts, jewelry was still a symbol of rank and social status, worn particularly by men and brides. Moslems of means freely purchased vast quantities of jewelry – crafted by others – with no apparent pangs of guilt.

Our people did not need to feel guilty either about creating or wearing beautiful jewelry. Indeed, the name of Betzalel, the supreme craftsman in stonecutting as well as metalwork and wood-carving, means "in the shadow of God." Betzalel was under His protection while constructing the *Mishkan* and the breastplate for the High Priest with its twelve precious gemstones – the *avnei milu'im* engraved with the names of the twelve tribes of

Israel. Amulets and talismen had always been sought for protection in the Jewish life cycle, and they were rendered as beautiful as possible as a fitting receptacle for sacred verses written with special care. Also, as a Jewish husband's wealth increased, it was incumbent upon him to adorn his wife suitably for their status.

In Yemen, I had often watched my father make an amulet case – which he called a *k'tab* – from silver, or even from gold for a wealthy client. In Jerusalem, Ezra had used cheaper materials, but he had also made them of great beauty with granulated filigree and clusters of small silver bells suspended from loops at the base. I still had a stock of scrolls to place in them that he had ordered from a *sofer*. They bore the Priestly Benediction:

May the Lord bless you and keep you.
May the Lord make His face to shine upon you
and be gracious unto you.
May the Lord lift up His countenance upon you
and give you peace.

However, there were very few amulet cases left and I knew I had to work hard to replenish the stock as these were among the most popular items. Earrings were also in demand. I had learned to construct these quickly, with pleasing design and harmony. Some designs were large and intricate, but they were lightweight because they were hollow. Although Ezra had often told me that mine were frequently more attractive than his, to the trained eye his work was far more skilled. I would adorn them with tiny seed pearls, which the tourists loved.

Sometimes my customers were very important people, like Adalbert, the prince of Prussia. The whole Rova buzzed with excitement when he came to visit

Jerusalem – it was not often that a personage of his stature appeared. The subject did not particularly interest me until one afternoon, when this tall, forbidding man in an impressive uniform embellished with many strands of gold braid, entered my shop, flanked by three naval officers. I was too flustered even to greet him, especially when he clicked his heels and bowed to me formally.

"May I speak with your husband?" he inquired.

"My...my husband p-passed away last year," I stammered, then I forced myself to calm down so that I would not appear to be a fool.

He pointed to the jewelry displayed in boxes lined in black velvet. "Whose work is this?"

"Most of it is mine," I replied in a more natural voice. "A few pieces of my husband's still remain.

He picked up a gold pendant portraying an eagle. "And who made this?"

"My late husband. He was very talented."

"It is very fine work," he acknowledged. "And these?" The prince indicating some spherical silver earrings with granulated loops.

"Those are mine," I admitted shyly.

"Indeed." He examined them closely. "Where did you learn your craft?"

"From my husband, mostly, but my father is also a great artisan," I added proudly.

"And he helps you?"

"Alas, he is still in Yemen. His masters will not let him leave."

"Why is that? Is he a criminal?"

My cheeks were flaming. I drew myself up erect. "My father is one of the most respected men in Sana'a," I declared. "The Moslems keep him there because his work is so beautiful, that they insist he train their apprentices."

The prince nodded. "How long has it been since you saw him last?"

"Nine years – since we left Yemen," I replied, tears filling my eyes.

Adalbert's voice softened. "Tell my officer here his name and address, so that he can write it down. Perhaps I can help."

"I will write it," I said, hastily grabbing a pen and paper. "Oh, you write too?" he commented. "Quite an accomplished lady."

He asked the price of the items he had indicated and said he would take them. Then he turned to his men. "Do you see anything you like – for your wives or lady friends, perhaps?"

All three of them chose earrings and one also bought an armlet for his daughter which I had made as an experiment. They did not flinch at the justifiably high price I quoted. They had instinctively chosen my best pieces, ones which represented many hours of work and would take me a long time to replace.

As I was wrapping them carefully in tissue paper, I listened to their conversation. Although they spoke among themselves in German, I found that, because of its similarity to the Yiddish I had learned from my friend Sarah, I was able to understand most of what they said. It seemed that their ship, the *S.M.S. Charlotte,* was visiting all the eastern Mediterranean ports. Nothing they said was particularly important, but I was thrilled that I had added yet another language to those that I either spoke or understood. Even if he would not have said so openly, I knew that Ezra would have been proud of me.

I handed the packages to one of the officers. Again Prince Adalbert clicked his heels. "The Turkish governor of Jerusalem, Jawad Pasha, is my host this evening for dinner. I shall speak to him about your father" were his parting words.

I could not wait to tell the children what had transpired. Could it be that the sun might shine again, even for me?

12

IT WAS TWO YEARS
BEFORE I received word that my
beloved father would soon be coming to
Jerusalem. To this day I do not know how it
came about – nor did he – but I like to think that
Prince Adalbert kept his word and set the process in
motion. It was only then that I learned that my mother,
with all her kindness and wisdom, had passed away. I
had known that her health was failing, but convinced
myself that the moment she would set foot on Holy Soil
she would be restored. She would see her grandchildren,
and her children who lived in other cities and settlements,
and she would regain the strength of her youth. But this
was not to be.

Since the sad news of her passing arrived more than
a year after the traditional *shivah* period, I observed only
the required symbolic mourning and would not allow
myself to sink into the sorrowful state that had followed
Ezra's death. I had too many responsibilities, and also
preparations to make for Abba's imminent arrival.

In the meantime, my facility with languages was
proving very valuable in the Holy City and for the first
time I consciously set my mind to acquiring skills in other
tongues. Even the languages I could not yet speak, I
quickly learned to understand, a gift which drew many
diverse people to my store. Some of them just wanted a
sympathetic ear someone to talk to – but most of them
bought jewelry from me and the business flourished.
Never able to turn away a potential customer, I found

myself keeping much longer hours than I had ever intended, and the strain was beginning to tell. I had less time than I would have liked for the children, and none for myself.

One evening, as I was doing the accounts, a partial solution presented itself. I saw, as I added and re-added the figures, that my financial position was no longer tenuous; I could afford to limit my shop hours to those observed by other businesses, that is, to close down the store between one and four in the afternoon each day. During those hours, I would make new pieces to replenish the stock. On Tuesdays I would not reopen at all after the break, but spend those hours purchasing raw materials from my suppliers. And every evening I would reserve for the children. I was very pleased with this arrangement, and grateful to the Almighty for His bounty that had made it possible.

Even under this new arrangement, I still did not take holidays, except for Shabbat and Festivals. But one day Sarah persuaded me to close the shop and have a *tiyul* – an outing, to tour the Jewish Quarter and some of the new neighborhoods outside the Old City walls. I had done so well the previous week, praise God, that I felt I could indulge myself this once.

Perhaps it is surprising that Sarah was my closest friend, considering that she was a generation older, but I always felt comfortable with her. Every meeting was a learning experience and she was never condescending or patronizing. She took it as a matter of course that because I had never had the opportunity to go to school, I could not be expected to know such things as history or geography. The skills I did have or managed to acquire evoked endless compliments from her, and when she criticized me, I always knew it was constructive criticism.

Unlike Yifat who found my widowhood devastating, Sarah understood that I did not want another husband; she never tried to convince me that I'd be better off to remarry.

The sun was shining in a cloudless blue sky the day of our outing and, as we walked through the Old City, Sarah pointed out the different settlers we passed, identifying them by their language and attire. "It's an ethnic mosaic, Mazal," she remarked. "You can stand on any corner in Jerusalem and in the space of ten minutes you'll see dozens of different costumes and hear as many languages – even more than you've managed to master!"

She pointed out a group of Bukharan Jews who had recently returned to Jerusalem and had already founded a vigorous community. "They were driven from Eretz Yisrael more than 2,000 years ago," Sarah noted. "How wonderful that they kept their religious traditions and culture."

"Every Jew wants to live in Eretz Yisrael," I commented.

She shook her head. "No, my dear. Some only want to come here to *die*. The Mount of Olives is covered with the graves of Jews who lived their lives in the *Golah* and dreamed of breathing their last on holy air. But those who do come here to live think they're coming to a Land flowing with milk and honey, as Hashem promised. Yet, even when they find out it's mostly barren, desolate and poverty-stricken, they still stay. That's the miracle of it!"

"Perhaps they, and we, and others who return to the Holy Land, will make it flow with milk and honey once again," I said, to which my friend added, "Yes, may it be His will."

As we strolled along, Sarah began to deliver a fascinating history lesson and I, her ever-avid student, clung to her every word. She told me that the great scholar Ramban – Rabbi Moshe ben Nachman – was among the first to include settling in Eretz Yisrael as one of the 613 Torah commandments. "He was a noted physician in Spain," she said, "and in the thirteenth century he was chosen to represent the Jews in a debate before King James of Aragon. Even though he won – or, more likely, *because* he won – he was expelled from the country and came to Jerusalem at the age of seventy-two. Can you imagine having to start all over again, in a foreign land, at that age? But the lives of Jews in the Diaspora have always been and always will be precarious. They might enjoy a period of relative security, and then anti-Semitism and persecution rise up once more and their peaceful lives are shattered.

"In every generation," Sarah went on, "when the suffering grew – as it inevitably did – Jews began to long for Redemption, for Mashiach."

"Yes," I agreed, "that is the way it was in Yemen. Of course, in our prayers we always spoke of the Redemption, the coming of Mashiach and the return to Tziyon, but when conditions in Sana'a worsened these words became much more meaningful. The people began to plan – not only to speak."

Sarah nodded and continued: "In the seventeenth century, European Jews' longing for Mashiach became very great after a wave of persecution and destruction. Do you know about the Chmielnicki massacres? Russian and Polish Jewry were the victims. They turned their hopes of salvation to Shabtai Tzvi, who claimed he was Mashiach. He amassed quite a following before he was unmasked as a false messiah. The persecution did not cease, and even today we hear about the terrible conditions abroad. Like Rabbi Yehudah He-Chasid, Rabbi Chaim

Malach, and Rabbi Avraham Ravigo and their disciples, many more will come, of that I am certain, to await Mashiach in the Holy Land."

"I will bring your seed from the east, and gather you from the west...," I said, quoting from the Prophet Yeshayahu, *"I will say to the North 'Give up!' and to Teiman 'Keep not back!' Bring My sons from afar and My daughters from the end of the earth."*

"Mazal, every word of the prophecies is true," Sarah said with feeling. "We need only be patient and we will see their fulfillment with our own eyes."

We continued strolling and Sarah continued her history lesson. She told me that the leaders of the Chasidic movement also considered settlement in Eretz Yisrael an important part of their philosophy. "The Chasidim came here in waves – the brother-in-law of the Baal Shem Tov was among the first, in the mid-1700s. Twenty years later, Rabbi Menachem Mendel Primishlaner and Rabbi Nachman Horodanker came, followed by the disciples of Rabbi Menachem Mendel of Vitebsk and Rabbi Avraham Kolisker. In the third wave came the Chabad Chasidim, who arrived, I think, around 1820."

Sarah noticed that I was having a bit of trouble absorbing so much information. "Your head must be swimming from all these strange names and places, Mazal! But I have one for you that I believe will not be so strange: The Baal Shem Tov's brother-in-law, Rabbi Avraham Gershon of Kutow, had an outstanding study partner – Rav Sar Shalom Sharabi."

"Morenu Sar Shalom of Yemen?!" I exclaimed. My eyes filled with tears. I had been feeling so...so inferior, I suppose, hearing about all those Ashkenazi scholars. Like an outsider, or someone lacking in merit. "Sarah, I saw a wall plaque on the *beit midrash* of Chasidim Mekubalim

Beit El that said Rabbi Gershon had learned there. Is that where he and *Morenu* Sar Shalom studied together?"

"Yes, my dear. The very place."

I hugged her impulsively. "Thank you, Sarah, thank you!" I cried. *"Morenu* Sar Shalom Sharabi was one of the greatest *Chachamim* my people has even known! I didn't think anyone here had even heard of him!" My dear friend had restored my pride and had given me a true sense of belonging.

"My throat is dry from talking," Sarah said. "Why don't you tell me something about Yemen? What was it like there? And were your family always jewelers?"

"For four generations," I told her. "But the real occupation of all Yemenite men is and always has been the study of the Holy Torah. It is because the community has been kept so poor by the Imam that even our *Chachamim* must soil their hands with physical labor – we cannot afford even to support them and their families. But it was not always so."

"Please, Mazal, tell me more," Sarah implored, genuinely interested.

"I heard this from my father, when I was a child," I began. "I believe it to be true, and people in Sana'a always spoke of it as though it was, but I cannot say for certain whether it is our history or a legend. Jews came to Yemen from the Exile of Babylonia, my father told me, and lived there in peace for hundreds of years, until the rise of Islam. In the twelfth century the Jews were caught in the crossfire of a war between the Caliph Saladin and the Shi'ites, who rebelled against his rule, and the Caliph held the Jews to blame for his misfortunes.

"Like the Jews of Europe and Russia, as you have said," I continued, "our people suffered terrible persecution, and in Yemen too a false messiah arose. He claimed that the Jews were destined to adopt the faith of Islam, and he showed them many proofs for this in the *Tanach. Mori* Yaakov ben Netanel al-Fayoumi did not believe this false messiah, although very many Jews did, and so he wrote to Rabi Moshe ben Maimon in Egypt, to ask him what our people were to do."

"Ah, so that is when the Rambam sent his famous *Iggeret!*" Sarah's eyes lit up with recognition.

"Yes," I said, "that is what my father said. The Rambam directed us from afar and he became our revered leader. For all matters of the Halachah, the Rambam was our judge and our guide.

"When the rebellion was finally put down, the Jews returned to their former peaceful state and flourished until two or three centuries ago. Then there was a blood libel – a crime against the Calipha for which a court Jew was held responsible. The Caliph banished all the Jews to the desert of Tahomey, where our people endured very severe hardships. The climate and conditions caused countless numbers to die. In addition, we suffered the loss of our *kitvei Kodesh* – our ancient sacred scrolls, as well as our silver and gold Torah ornaments, and our beautiful houses of prayer. The legacy of a thousand years or more was lost.

"While our people were in the desert, the Caliph suffered too, for there were plagues and pestilence in the land. He believed he was being punished by Allah for exiling the Jews, and so he allowed our people to return, but not to the city of Sana'a. He set aside El Kabir al-Azav for Jewish settlement, and there they built their homes."

"I suppose they were permitted to return eventually to Sana'a, is that right?"

"Yes, Sarah, but many restrictions were imposed on

the community. We were forbidden to wear new clothes, or even old ones if they were finely made and sewn with threads of gold and silver. We were barred from riding donkeys or mules, even for long journeys. And we could not engage in businesses except as artisans and metalworkers. The Moslems are too lazy and ignorant for that sort of work.

"But despite our labor, Sarah, we never ceased learning Torah. The family of *Mori* Yosef ben Saadi, for example, were blacksmiths. *Mori* Yosef knew all of Torah and Talmud and Rambam, as well as the Zohar and the writings of the Ari. He would hold an iron horseshoe or farm implement with his tongs over the fire while his father, Sa'id, operated the bellows and his younger brother wielded the hammer. The clanging of metal against the anvil was like music that accompanied the lyrics of Torah, which the three men sang as they worked."

"Oh, Mazal, that is a beautiful story. Tell me, my dear, have you never had new clothing, never known a moment of real ease in all your young life?"

I looked at my companion and wondered if I could ever explain to her the true beauty of our community in Sana'a. Could she understand what it meant in Yemen to live the double life of a Jew – where we dressed in finery inside our simple homes when we welcomed the Shabbat and the Festivals? I did not have the words to describe the royal gown I had worn at my Chinah, or the exquisite ark that held the Torah scroll in our *beit knesset.*

"Ease?" I said, echoing Sarah's words. "Ease is knowing that the hooves of Moslem horses will not trample my children and my home. Ease is knowing that the Almighty cradles us in the palm of His Hand in His Holy City. Ease, my dearest Sarah, is having you for a friend."

We sat down to rest in the shade for a bit and Sarah and I discussed a book she had recently lent me. She was so proud of my literary skills that she kept encouraging me to read more books, especially ones that had been published by her famous Bak family. Sarah, in her usual floral cotton frock and strong black boots, listened attentively as I recited a passage describing Rabbi David Yellin's journey to Israel:

We left Constantinople and sailed for ten days.

Suddenly there came a strong wind and a mighty storm such that we thought the ship would shatter. We lay down like corpses in the hold. We felt as if we were borne on eagle's wings, ascending mountains and descending into valleys. Thus it continued for two days and nights. Suddenly we felt that the ship had come to a halt and the sailors cast anchor. We rejoiced greatly, for we thought we had reached the destination of our desire, the City of Acre. How keen was our regret and disappointment when we ascended and saw that we had docked again at Constantinople. We had retraced the entire ten-day distance in only two days and nights because of the mighty east wind which propelled our ship. Several days passed and the ship became ready to set out once again. After another thirty days of nearly fatal torture, we finally did arrive at Acre.

Sarah clapped her hands with delight. "My little friend," she said in wonder, "what other hidden talents do you possess?"

"None, I'm afraid," I answered shyly. "I memorize

as much as I can from your books because I am afraid that the new facts I read about will escape from me, and I'll revert to being the ignorant girl who arrived in Jerusalem a decade ago."

Sarah was silent for a while. "I think," she said after a pause, "that if you'd been born in a different place, perhaps in a different time, you could have been a great scholar or perhaps played a role in the history of this country."

I blushed and hurriedly arose from our shady spot. Sarah followed. The sun beat down on us as we walked, but we paid no heed. "I'm serious, Mazal," Sarah pressed.

"But I'm just a woman...," I began.

Sarah shook her head. "Chavah was just a woman – the mother of all creation. Sarah, Rivkah, Rachel, and Leah were all just women. Devorah the Prophetess was just a woman. I don't think you realize how remarkable you are."

"I know a little bit," I conceded, "but it's just a drop in the ocean of knowledge. You know so much more."

"Mazal, you're like a sponge. You soak up everything, every bit of information. What.can I possibly tell you that you don't already know?"

"I want to know how the Jews came to Jerusalem, where they came from." In Sana'a we had not known there were other Jews in *every* part of the world, and those we did know about, we thought were exactly like us! For Sarah, this was like mother's milk. In her household of learned men, such topics were dinner-table conversation and her children studied them in school. My own ignorance was abysmal.

Ever patient, Sarah explained to me how, despite the hardships, great scholars continued to come. "They came even from Baghdad, the families of Shlomo

Yechezkel Yehudah and Eliyahu Mani. They and their
disciples settled in Chevron in 1860. A few years later
Avraham Moshe Lunz came to Jerusalem with his parents
– he was just bar-mitzvah age then and he grew to be an
extraordinary Rav even though he was blind."

"I knew a blind scholar in Sana'a," I interjected. "He
was called Ovadiah Gaon." I reminisced for a moment
about this brilliant teacher who would deliver *derashot*
on Shabbat to a gathering of Jews silenced and awestruck
by his words. "I'm sorry for interrupting, Sarah," I said.
"Please go on."

The history lesson now moved to a new geographical
location, western Asia, where the Jews learned of Eretz
Yisrael through emissaries sent from the Holy Land –
shelichim who were charged with the duty of fostering
the aliyah of Bukharan Jews.

"Oh, yes," I said, "like those we saw earlier, in the
colorful clothing and the squarish *kippot.*"

"Interestingly, the Bukharan *kehillah,* which has
always been very pious, followed the *nusach Ashkenaz*
for prayers. But the *shelichim* apparently convinced the
community to adopt *nusach Sefard,* and they have done
so ever since. When a sufficient number of Bukharan Jews
had arrived," Sarah said, "they founded their own quarter
in Jerusalem – a very elegant neighborhood with spacious
homes and flowering courtyards.

"Then Georgian Jews began to arrive in Jerusalem
during the 1860s, and they too constructed a new
neighborhood for themselves outside the Old City walls,
near the Damascus Gate." We were nearing this area and
would soon be able to see it for ourselves.

"Next came the Jews from the Caucasus, led by
Rabbi Yaakov Yitzchak of Darband. And then *your*
people, Mazal," Sarah said.

This, at least, was a subject I knew well. "We were inspired by the Torah verse in the Song of Solomon: 'I have said that I shall ascend the date palm.' The word *b'tamar* in *gematria* is equivalent to 642. Our *chachamim* taught that this number was our Redemption sign – in 5642, the Jews would be redeemed, and we all wanted to be here in Eretz Yisrael for the *Geulah.* Since Ezra and I arrived, the number of Yemenite Jews in Jerusalem has grown to 400. Do you know, we had to be granted permission to leave by the Vizier Kaima Kain. He even posted a royal decree with the Jews mentioned by name. Like Pharaoh in Egypt, he had changed his mind several times, but by now most of the Jews in our community who were fit to travel have come. I'm sure the rest will follow eventually."

By the time we reached the Damascus Gate, I had also learned that among the earliest *Chovevei Tziyon,* "lovers of Zion," were Rabbi Yehudah ben Shlomo Chai Alkalai and Rabbi Tzvi Hirsch Kalischer, who also inspired many followers to settle with them in Jerusalem. Rabbi Kalischer was the Rav of Thorn, Posen and the author of *Derishat Tziyon,* in which he wrote: "The Redemption will come about through the natural process of mass aliyah and settlement of the Land of Israel. We must increase the number of people in the Holy Land and ensure that it is densely populated with Jews."

We still had a long way to go before his words would be fulfilled, but things had certainly improved in the past decade. The years to come would surely bring great changes, and with the Almighty's help, many more diaspora Jews would come. For now, Sarah and I were simply enjoying our leisurely afternoon, absorbing the sights and sounds of our beloved city.

13

NOT ONLY GREAT RABBIS
and scholars were arriving in Jerusalem.
The Jewish Quarter was abuzz with the news
that a young religious doctor named Moshe
Wallach, only twenty-six years old, had made aliyah.
It had come about because thirty years ago, "Anshei Hod,"
the group of public-minded Jews from Germany and
Holland who had built the Battei Machaseh, initiated
another vital project: they sent two emissaries abroad –
Yaakov Libes Levi and Yoel Moshe Solomon – to raise
funds for the construction of a modern Jewish hospital
which would serve all the sick of Jerusalem, regardless
of race or religion, and at the same time counteract the
missionary activities of the Christian hospitals. Although
two small Jewish hospitals had opened in the intervening
years – Bikur Cholim and Misgav Ladach – the
emissaries' efforts were successful, and this young doctor
would be Director of the new facility. The Kaiser's
ambassador in Constantinople, Radolitz, and the German
consul in Jerusalem, Dr. von Tischendorf, had persuaded
the Turkish authorities to give their consent and waive
the property tax.

While the hospital was being built, Dr. Wallach
opened a free outpatient clinic and pharmacy in the Old
City. His reputation grew day by day. How I wished he
had come in time to save my Ezra! I still felt unbearable
guilt that by delaying taking him to the hospital I had
contributed to his death. Sarah grew angry with me when
I said this and pointed out that hundreds – even those

who had gone to the hospital – had succumbed to influenza, cholera, malaria and typhoid at that time. "In the final analysis, Mazal," she added, "we both know that these things are in the Almighty's hands!" The new hospital which Dr. Wallach would head, to be named *Shaare Zedek* – "the Gates of Righteousness" – was to be constructed a twenty-minute cart ride away, two miles from the Old City on Jaffa Road.

News traveled fast in the Rova and soon we knew all about the young doctor: he was a bachelor (a fact that gave hope to many women with unmarried daughters, but the story went that he had vowed never to marry), one of seven children of a textile trader in Cologne. Dr. Wallach was welcomed with great delight, and he did not disappoint us. He was indefatigable, working all day in his clinic and pharmacy, and at night, with a lantern in his hand, he would walk the dark, narrow roads of the Old City to treat the poor in their homes.

Sometimes if one of the children had a fever, I would also send for the new doctor, no longer putting all my faith in the herbal remedies. Because my little Ruchama, now aged nine, loved the garden so, I passed on to her all that my mother had taught me about herbs and allowed her to tend the plants herself. At the same time, however, I warned her that serious illness needed modern medicine and potent drugs.

Sarah and I continued to stroll contentedly. Our footsteps soon brought us to the new neighborhood outside the Damascus Gate, and happily I revisited Mishkenot Sha'ananim, where my family and Yifat's had once considered settling. Finally we took a carriage to Kfar Shiloach, to spend some time with Yifat. I had brought with me all kinds of pastries, *malawach* and *f'tut*, knowing she would want to offer us refreshments but couldn't afford to. There was sufficient food in my basket to satisfy her large family as well, may Hashem watch over them. I also wanted to give her some money, if I could find a way of doing it without hurting her pride. As we settled in at her house, an idea occurred to me.

"Yifat," I asked, "do you have perhaps some embroidery to sell me? I feel I must have more variety to offer the tourists besides my jewelry."

Diffidently she brought out her work, which I knew she had been trying to sell for some time. It was exquisite! In traditional Yemenite style, she had stitched many patterns with silver and gold thread in circular and filigree shapes. She had made some children's dresses with embroidered yokes and trim around the hem and sleeves, as well as unusual challah and matzah covers embroidered with silk threads. She had sewn motifs of birds, flowers, the six-pointed Star of David, and even fruits of the Holy Land, beautiful decorations of pomegranates, grapes, olives and dates.

Sarah echoed my lavish praise of her craftsmanship. "I'll take them all!" I said rashly, wondering if I'd even have enough room to display them. I offered her a large sum of money.

Yifat's eyes widened with disbelief. "Are you sure?" she whispered, stunned at the windfall.

"Some of the dresses will be for Ruchama," I replied, "and the rest for the shop. I'm certain I will make a handsome profit." My air of confidence was convincing but in truth I did not have the faintest idea if I could sell any of them.

Yifat was too overcome to speak. "I will need a lot more," I told her. "Can you supply me regularly?" I used my best business voice, hiding the profound emotion I felt at seeing her eyes fill with tears.

She nodded speechlessly. As she packed up her embroidery for me, I discreetly left the money on the table. At least I knew that her family would have chicken and wine on the table for quite a few Shabbatot to come.

The news of my father's imminent arrival pushed me into a decision I had been weighing for a long time. Sarah told me that a house had been put up for sale at the Chosh where she lived. It was situated just west of the north end of Chabad Street, adjacent to the Sukkat Shalom courtyard of Rabbi Yeshaya Bardaki. I had always loved the Chosh. To me it was the most fashionable and exotic part of the Rova and I knew this residential courtyard would be much healthier for the children. Where we now lived, near the Ashpot Gate, we continually inhaled the stench of garbage, as this was still its exit from the city. The other consideration was space: Ruchama was too big to go on sharing a room with her brothers, and I would need a place also for Abba when he came.

I was amazed that I had saved enough to buy the house Sarah mentioned, and could even afford to keep our present home just as a workshop and store. At the Chosh I would have three rooms atop a broad staircase spilling over with ivy, with a nice patch of garden below. There was a carob tree and an orange tree that perfumed the air with sweetness when it was in blossom. The two boys could share a room, Ruchama would share my bedroom, and one whole room could be our salon. That way, Abba, who was very independent, could have our present home all to himself.

My mind filled with ideas now that moving had become a reality. The store could be expanded to two rooms, as Abba would only need one room for himself. Moving the workshop to the back would leave the front room just for the store and I had some wonderful plans for making it attractive for the tourists who flocked to the Old City from all over the world. There would even be space for Yifat's exquisite Yemenite embroidery.

Sarah was delighted with my ideas. "You have come so far, Mazal," she said approvingly.

"It's only a short walk between the two dwellings," I answered naively.

Sarah laughed. "I mean from the little girl who arrived here from Yemen – was it really only ten years ago? When I mentioned then how young you were, you protested that you were not a child but a married woman. Yes, a married woman, and not even fifteen years of age.

I nodded. Everything is relative. My own daughter would be fifteen in just six years, and in Yemen would be eligible for marriage in only three. But this was not the custom in Jerusalem and I was glad of it now. I wanted her to freely have the education that I had been forced to acquire surreptitiously. Like all mothers, I wanted her life to be easier than mine. Yet I couldn't wish her a kinder husband than Ezra had been to me. I knew that as soon as Abba arrived, the subject of Ruchama's marriage would be raised. He would talk to me about a *shidduch* for her with a boy from our own background when the time came, and he would want to begin planning her future well in advance.

I smiled to myself. Yifat's son, Evyatar, would be the ideal person, I thought. The two had played together as small children, and our families were close. I still loved this boy like my own son, remembering how I had cuddled him for comfort on our journey to Jerusalem, before I knew I myself was expecting a baby. Evyatar, although only ten now, already showed signs of being a sensible, strong boy like his father. Yes, one day my gentle, artistic daughter would wear the golden pomegranate pendant at her Chinah ceremony, carrying on the family tradition as my own mother would have wished.

Sarah would laugh at me, already making plans for my little girl. As close as we were, there were still many things about me she could not begin to understand. I nodded to myself... I would arrange everything.

14

MY BELOVED FATHER
ARRIVED not in a caravan of donkeys
and carts as we had done, but on the very
first train to steam into Jerusalem. The railway
from Jaffa to Jerusalem by way of Nachal Sorek has
just been completed. I wished that my Ezra had lived to
see these amazing developments. Before he died, an *Aron
Kodesh* from Kherson in Russia was carried from Jaffa
to Jerusalem on the backs of twelve camels. And now,
we not only had a railway, but I had heard that a Jewish
hotel, complete with stables and coffee house, had been
opened in Motza, just outside Jerusalem, for the
convenience of travelers.

The children had been excited for weeks and talked
ceaselessly of the grandfather whom they had never
known but who would soon be part of their lives. Yet,
when his small, frail figure stepped onto the platform
and I cried out in delight, they hung back, suddenly
speechless. He was dressed as I remembered him in
Yemen, in flowing robes, his long tightly-curled *payot,*
which had been black when I left Sana'a, now almost
white. He seemed to have shrunk – perhaps through grief
over my mother's death, or perhaps I had always thought
of him as larger than life.

We both cried as we embraced. Then he held me at
arm's length, gazing in wonder at this grown, mature
daughter whom he hadn't seen for ten years.

I was suddenly terribly self-conscious. Long ago, I
had abandoned the traditional Yemenite attire that most

of my countrymen still wore, because I sensed it made my customers uncomfortable. At first I adopted Sarah's simple style but with prosperity had come the ability to have more sophisticated outfits sewn by a skilled dressmaker. I had had a new ensemble made for this occasion and Abba's eyes took in every detail from my rust silk head covering to my cream-colored high-collared blouse, long brown skirt, and fashionable high-button shoes. Then his eyes fastened on the pomegranate pendant and he gave a little smile, as if to say: at last, something familiar, something with which he could identify. Perhaps it reassured him that I was still Mazal, still true in her heart to our Yemenite traditions despite the modern attire.

He put his hands on the heads of the three children and blessed them, each one repeating their name and age in case he didn't know. Ruchama's words were almost a whisper: "Djeddi, I am Ruchama and I'm ten." Shalom just held up six fingers, but Assaf spoke out in a very strong voice: "My name is Assaf and I'm eight, Djeddi."

Abba smiled. "Just like his father," he said to me. "Decisive. A good scholar?"

I nodded quickly. I was glad he hadn't asked me the same question about Shalom, who wanted to be outside playing all the time and gave me, and his teachers, a very hard time.

We went first to the house I had prepared for him, entering through the store and the workshop. Djeddi's eyes widened in disbelief. "You work for an Ottoman master?" he asked.

"Abba, it is mine. I own it. I would be honored if you could help me in the workshop – but, of course, only if it pleases you.

Djeddi's expression became very grim. "What nonsense you speak, daughter," he said with annoyance.

"It is impossible. Women do not own property..."

A lengthy, and sometimes heated, debate followed as I tried to explain how different things were and showed him my deeds and other documents. He still thought Ezra had exhibited unexpected foolhardiness in allowing my name to appear as co-proprietor and in imagining a mere woman could possibly manage a business. I soon realized that further discussion was fruitless; Djeddi would have to see for himself.

We toured the shop slowly, Djeddi carefully examining every item for quality of workmanship. "All this jewelry! Ezra left so much?" he asked in puzzlement.

"No, Abba. Ezra's work has long since been sold. I made this – all of it."

He sat down. I knew now that I should have prepared him better in my letters, but I was never boastful by nature and in any case, it would have been too hard for him to comprehend. I think he believed that I was living from *chalukah* – the tithe paid by pious Jews all over the world and distributed to their poor brethren in Jerusalem. Djeddi looked around the room I had prepared for him. "It is very grand, Mazal, but too small for the five of us. I will sleep in the workshop."

"Abba, this is just for you. I have another house, quite close."

He shook his head. Things were happening too fast. "Did you marry again and not tell me?" he asked.

"No, Abba. I bought the house myself, with savings from my earnings. The Almighty has been good to me. Please rest now and I will come in an hour or two to take you to my house to eat. In the meantime, there is a bowl of fruit here and *gisher* to drink."

I had not told him that my brothers and sisters had all come from their homes on moshavim in Petach Tikvah and Rishon l'Tziyon and were waiting to welcome him at the Chosh. Better for him to rest first before he had to make even more adjustments. One of my sisters, Shoshanna, had married an Ashkenazi farmer three years ago and she was still afraid to tell him.

As I prepared to leave, Djeddi said suddenly: "Mazal, you are too independent. I will arrange a *shidduch* for you with one of our countrymen soon."

"No, Abba, I don't want one. I don't need another husband."

"But you can have more children! Three is a very small family. You should have another girl and name her Miriam, after your mother."

"Shoshanna has a baby girl and she named her Miriam."

"Shoshanna is a mother?" he said wonderingly. "Did she marry one of the boys who came with her from Sana'a, or from a later aliyah?"

I swallowed and drew a deep breath. "She married a fine boy, Abba. His name is Yoel."

"From which village is he?"

"He comes from Poland, Abba."

Djeddi looked bewildered. "Not from Yemen!? Where does he learn? What is his craft?"

"He's a farmer, Abba, and a good Jew. He learns and his farm is run strictly according to Halachah. He is very good to Shoshanna and she loves him very much."

"Polish...Ashkenazi...farmer," he muttered. Djeddi was still shaking his head in confusion as I propelled the children out of the house.

We had a wonderful reunion, all the family together, and Djeddi met several new sons- and daughters-in-law as well as all his grandchildren. He was cordial even to

Yoel. But although he was not really old, he was a shadow of the man I remembered. The long yearning to reach Jerusalem had been fulfilled, but without his lifetime partner, the triumph seemed less sweet and his joy less spirited.

The whole way from the house near the Ashpot Gate to my new home in the Chosh, he was very quiet. Probably, like Ezra, he had been expecting a Jerusalem of gold, but many of the streets were unpaved and undrained and there was the ever-present stench of poor sanitation and signs of squalor. He said nothing of his disappointment, feeling it would be wicked to criticize the Holy City in any way.

The children quickly grew to love him. They needed a man in the family to replace their father, and they brought all their friends to see him in the workshop. Within a few days, he was helping me – unable to sit idle – and once he recovered from his bewilderment over my being a silversmith, he not only praised my work but showed me how to improve it. We felt like a family again, drawn closer together because of the losses we had both sustained. Only once more did he bring up the subject of my remarriage.

"It is three years now you have been without a husband. It is long enough for a young woman."

"Abba, do you wish to marry again?"

He looked shocked. "I? Of course not, Mazal. Never! I never wanted another wife even when Imma was still alive, although many of my friends had two wives. My own father had two wives. But your mother was all I ever needed. Now that she is gone, may her soul dwell peacefully in *Gan Eden,* I still have no wish for any other woman. Besides, I am old."

"You're not so old, Abba. But you would not find

another like Imma, true?"

He nodded.

"I feel the same," I said gently. "Ezra was special. He let me grow and develop. We worked together. We shared a life. That only happens once. I know you of all people can understand."

Djeddi took my hand. "If that is how you feel, my daughter, it is good that I came. I think we need each other."

Abba's adjustment to Eretz Yisrael took quite some time. He had always been a leader of the community in Yemen, particularly in the area of religious affairs, and so many aspects of religious life in the Holy Land were hard for him to accept. Our *Chachamim* were not permitted to interpret halachah or pass on our traditions, and even our *shochetim* were suspect for *kashrut* in Jerusalem and barred from performing ritual slaughter of animals and fowl. We had to choose between following the customs of the Ashkenazi or Sefardi communities. Most of our people chose to join the Sefardim, as they couldn't speak or understand Yiddish. There were some advantages to this: Sefardi leaders were represented at the court of the sultan, which helped with exemption from the Turkish army and, since the Turks also ruled in Yemen, we could more easily – through Sefardi connections – maintain contact with relatives still in Sana'a.

Although the Jewish community had treated us with suspicion at first, we gradually won their respect because of our piety and scholarship, our initiative and industriousness – even in agriculture or stone-cutting. Our people had worked with Moslems in Yemen and spoke fluent Arabic, so they were not afraid to contact Arab builders from Bethlehem to ask for work, even though they were unaccustomed to hard physical labor and suffered from the heat.

Many of my countrymen were very poor and, like Yifat's family, had moved outside the walls, especially to Kfar Shiloach. At least Yifat and Reuven had a house there, humble as it was. Other Yemenite Jews were living in open fields or in caves. Without telling anyone, I would send money to them before the Festivals, asking Reuven to deliver it to them from "a friend overseas in rich America." In a way it was true: without the wealthy tourists, many of whom were indeed American, I would not have been able to do it.

When Djeddi got over the shock of my owning two properties, he admitted to being very proud of me. "Mazal, you did well," he would tell me, "because when you redeem the Land, you are also redeemed. By buying land in Eretz Yisrael, you have assured a place for your family in the World to Come."

"And with the Almighty's help, as long as visitors continue to flock to Jerusalem, I'll be able to assure my family's place in this world as well."

Of all the visitors, the most comical by far had been a group of English tourists. Thomas Cook, a British travel agent and Baptist preacher, had launched his "Eastern Tours" by bringing an upper-middle-class group here, to camp outside the walls. There they were served English tea and crumpets on tables laid with starched white linen and fine silverware, and their tents were carpeted. Although the Jewish Quarter residents doubled up with laughter whenever they talked about them, I had no complaints: many of them had visited our shop and bought brooches and pendants, as well as some of Yifat's embroidered dresses, to take back to England as a great novelty.

Now that the children were growing older and

becoming more independent, I had far more time to be a gracious saleswoman. With Djeddi making much of the jewelry (which he insisted on doing as his way of "paying for his keep,") I could really take time to interest customers in our wares. The Europeans particularly seemed to love my explanations about the amulets and the symbols that we etched or embossed on the jewelry. The piece that drew the most admiration, however, was always my own pomegranate pendant. When they asked if they could buy it or have it copied, I would simply shake my head. Like my marriage, it was "one of a kind" – never to be duplicated.

15

LIFE HAD BECOME much
easier for me since Djeddi had come to
Jerusalem. Not only did he help me with the
jewelry making, but he also helped me bring up
the three children – not an easy task. They were so
different from one another that each required individual
handling, and there were many times I would have been
in despair had I not had my father's wisdom to guide me.
True, Sarah remained a good and constant friend, but she
was, after all, Ashkenazi and could not be expected to
know our Yemenite traditions which I was anxious to
preserve as much as possible.

Ruchama was nearly seventeen – I had been a mother
of two at her age, but the custom was different here. She
was beautiful in appearance and in nature, with mahogany
skin, large brown eyes fringed with long lashes and jet
black hair that cascaded in waves to her waist. She still
liked to dress in very light colors, just as she had as a
small child, when she had wanted to wear only white.
Soon she would finish her studies at the Evelina de
Rothschild Girls' School.

I must digress here to mention a still painful incident
that occurred some years ago, when Ruchama completed
elementary school. All of the Ashkenazi girls in the Rova
who continued their studies – and there were not many –
attended the same school. But my Ruchama was not
accepted there. There had been no difficulty placing the
boys in yeshivot, but Ruchama, so undeniably "different,"
had been turned away. Even Sarah's great influence could

not breach the barrier of prejudice. And so, reluctantly, I enrolled my daughter at Evelina, a religious institute but more modern than I would have liked.

Now a young lady, Ruchama was like a delicate butterfly and my heart ached that her father had not lived to see her grow up. She was not very practical and I never thought to ask her to work in the shop, although she was quite talented and painted beautifully. Sometimes we sold one of her watercolors for her. They were unusual glimpses of Jerusalem captured by an artist in love with her subject: a courtyard with a clay urn from which crimson blossoms overflowed; little boys with long, curled payot learning Gemara together; the skyline of the Old City against the pearly dawn or at sunset, as the shadows lengthened in silver and indigo.

Ruchama wrote poetry too and composed her own melodies. Sarah's youngest, son, Menachem, had learned to play the violin as a child and Sarah often gave him a piece Ruchama had written, He would play these soul-stirring tunes while we all listened with tears in our eyes. Now aged twenty, Menachem played the kind of Jewish music born in the villages of Russia and Europe, and Ruchama still enjoyed hearing him play. His family, our close neighbors in the Chosh, was like an extension of our own.

Ruchama's music was different – haunting and sad, yet exquisitely beautiful. Under Menachem's nimble fingers, her melodies soared to rapturous heights and then almost seemed to whisper. She still did not have many close friends apart from the Bak-Levy family, Yifat's children, and a few classmates, but it never worried her. She still enjoyed solitude and never tired of walking around the Old City and the new neighborhoods that were springing up outside the gates.

She would often go on errands for me with Assaf, now fifteen, to Meah She'arim. He had many friends in this religious suburb who learned with him at his yeshivah. It was a paradox that the very pious families of Meah She'arim, led by Reb Zalman, had hired as their architect a German-born missionary named Conrad Schick. He had originally come to Jerusalem as an agent of the London Society for the Propagation of the Gospel Among the Jews. However, he soon halted his missionary activities and became very fond of the Jewish people. They in turn admired his work: contiguous row houses built around the periphery of the site. The backs of the houses were turned outwards, making a defensive wall with gates that could be closed at night. They all had an interior courtyard with water cisterns and there were also synagogues and *mikvaot*. Sarah told me that Meah She'arim felt comfortable to these families because it was not dissimilar in style and character to the Eastern European ghettoes from which they had emerged, even though they had not consciously attempted to adopt that pattern.

Ruchama also loved to visit the new Bukharan Quarter with her brothers and often took her sketchbook. It had wide streets and spacious houses, and one luxurious building called Ha-Armon – "the Palace." It looked like an Italian Renaissance villa and it was said that the wealthy builders hoped it would be used by Mashiach when he arrived in Jerusalem.

Just as Ruchama was a dreamer, Assaf was a scholar – as Ezra had predicted. The men in my family had always worked in addition to learning Torah, and sometimes it worried me that Assaf was not being prepared in his yeshivah for any livelihood. I turned to Djeddi for advice.

"Abba, am I doing the right thing?" I asked him. "Ezra said that Assaf should just learn unless I needed for him to earn money to help support the family. But, praise God, we have a good *parnassah.* What if one day the tourism and our income cease? Is it honorable that if we do not teach him a trade, one day he may have to live from *chalukah?*"

Djeddi patted my hand. "It would not be so terrible, Mazal. I listened to a *shiur* by Rav Yosef Chaim Sonnenfeld on this very subject. He said that the Yishuv is like an army stationed away from home to defend its nation's interests. Just as troops are entitled to be supported by their nation, so our young men who devote their lives to learning should be supported by Jews all over the world so they may continue their holy, blessed work. In truth, Assaf can do many things. If need be, he can work as a scribe or a teacher. Do not worry, my daughter. If you need a worker, his brother will work," Djeddi added, shaking his head. "Shalom was not meant to be a scholar."

It seemed that Ezra had possessed prophetic vision. He had warned me that Shalom would be difficult. At the recent celebration of his bar mitzvah, Shalom had not made us very proud in the *beit knesset.* For him, learning was a burden to be avoided at all costs. He was bright, but books bored him. Always the sun and the birds outside beckoned; there were boys to meet and games to play. Every year we waited for him to outgrow his restlessness, knowing deep inside it would not happen. He had no interest in becoming a silversmith either. Many were the discussions I had with him that invariably began with: "Shalom, what is to become of you?"

Sarah would chide me: "He is still a child. Give him time – he may yet surprise you." But, like my late husband, I knew it was something more. He even wanted to go off alone and live in Kfar Shiloach, near Yifat and Reuven.

Whenever we had one of our frequent arguments, he threatened to run away and live in a cave near the springs.

"Would it be so terrible, Imma?" he would argue. "Those are the springs that were the water source for the Sukkot celebration, *Simchat Beit Ha-shoevah,* in Temple times."

"It is also the place where Rabbi Yehudah He-Chasid came from Shedlitz to settle," I would reply acidly, "and when he immersed himself in the spring of Shiloach, a snake bit him and he died.

Shalom just laughed. "We have many Yemenite friends there, Imma. It is open to all of nature, not all closed-in stone like the Old City."

"It is open to all the elements – wind, and rain, and heat," I corrected him, "and our friends live there because they unfortunately cannot afford to live in a better, safer area. You have a nice home and a family here. Why can't you study and make something of yourself, try to be more like your brother Assaf."

"No, thank you. Assaf is good, too good, all the time – I can't stand it. And *I'm not Assaf!*"

The resentment Shalom felt towards his brother did not extend to Ruchama. Although she was sensitive and quiet while Shalom was boisterous and noisy, still he adored her. She had infinite patience with him and she was the only one in the family in whom he would confide. He wanted to leave his yeshiva and work with his hands – even as a farmer or a stonemason. I didn't know how to curb his wild spirit. He respected his grandfather, but Djeddi had no influence on him whatsoever. He would disappear for long periods of time with boys who were considered the rough element of the neighborhood. What *would* become of him? I prayed to the Almighty for guidance.

Ruchama's future, however, was clear. I never had any doubts that my plans for her would one day come to fruition. Djeddi and I had agreed that Yifat and Reuven's son, Evyatar, would be the ideal Yemenite husband for her and I had long ago discussed it with his parents. They too had thought it a match made in Heaven. It only remained for me to get Ruchama's consent.

"You'll soon be leaving school, my dear," I began. "It is time for you to marry."

Ruchama nodded. My smile widened. "Your childhood friend will be an excellent match for you, don't you agree?"

"Of course, Imma."

"It is true that his family does not have a lot of money, but fortunately I will be able to give you a sizable dowry and there will not be a problem. When should we arrange your Chinah ceremony?"

"I don't think I'll be having one."

"Not have one! What are you saying?" I cried indignantly. "Evyatar's family will also expect it!"

"Evyatar!? But Imma, I don't want to marry Evyatar. I want to marry my childhood friend Menachem. Sarah's son – Menachem Bak-Levy!"

16

I SAT DOWN ABRUPTLY,
for once in my life at a loss for words.
When I could speak, I said quietly:
"Ruchama, it's not possible."

"Why, Imma?" Her voice was cool. "You know
all the reasons as well as I do. We are Yemenite – it is
our background, our culture, our tradition."

"You don't think Menachem is a worthy young
man?"

"Of course I do. You know that. All of Sarah's
children are outstanding human beings, pious and talented
and good. But their tradition is Ashkenazi, ours is
Yemenite. It is a different world."

Ruchama remained composed. Her hands rested
lightly on her pale primrose silk skirt, while mine were
clenched, the knuckles showing white.

"Imma, do you believe that we live in the time of
the Ingathering of the Exiles?"

I nodded. All the signs seemed to indicate that this
was so.

"Do you believe that all the Jews are being brought
here from the four corners of the earth, to be planted
within their rightful borders?"

I nodded again, emotion choking me.

"This beautiful concept – is it not part of the Divine
plan?" She didn't wait for an answer. "Do you think God
would bring all the Jews together in one small place if
He did not want them to marry each other, be fruitful and
multiply? Do you think that some Jews are better than

115

others, maybe because we have dark skin and they are pale?"

My daughter was always clever, not only better educated than I but far more articulate.

"My objection has nothing to do with being better, but being different. Oil and water don't mix." I trotted out the old cliche' for lack of anything better.

She laughed. "Anyone would think I was suggesting marrying a Moslem, Heaven forbid. Imma, you know Menachem even better than Evyatar. Sarah has been your friend from the first day you came to Jerusalem. We live next door to one another. We are like one family. You see Evyatar perhaps every few weeks, but Menachem you see every day. He is my *zivug* – surely you see it too? We are like twin parts of one soul. He is a scholar, pious and dedicated. Like me, he loves music and all things beautiful. He has few friends, just as I do, preferring solitude and to commune with his Creator. What can you possible have against him?"

"I have nothing against him. I love him as a son...

"Then why not as a son-in-law?"

I searched my mind wildly. "He won't let you eat rice at Pesach," I suddenly blurted out.

Ruchama burst into such gales of laughter that after a few seconds I joined her, the battle lost. Then a sobering thought struck me. "You have it all planned in your mind, Ruchama, but perhaps this *shidduch* will not be good enough for his parents. They are descended from illustrious Torah scholars and will surely not wish to dilute their bloodline. Perhaps they have plans of their own for Menachem."

Ruchama smiled. "Sarah is very wise, Imma. She is very forward-thinking and she has seen for many years what has come as such a shock to you. There is no

Ashkenazi girl who would be as suitable a wife for her son as I would be."

I was silent, knowing that she was probably right. Sarah had very advanced ideas and no thought of racial prejudice would ever cross her mind. She had proved to me that some of my superstitions were un-Jewish adaptations of Moslem beliefs; perhaps my bias was also a remnant of Yemenite-Arab culture.

Suddenly another thought struck me. "Djeddi!"

At the mention of her grandfather, even Ruchama's complacency vanished. "We must find a way to tell him – you'll think of something, won't you, Imma?" Ruchama pleaded.

I loved my father very much, but on some subjects he was implacable. This was one of them. Although one of my sisters had married an Ashkenazi and he tolerated her marriage in a resigned way, I knew that if his beloved eldest granddaughter did the same, it would break his heart.

"I can't tell him," I said finally.

Ruchama looked frightened. "Perhaps Sarah will think of a way," she suggested.

"But Sarah knows nothing of your plans."

"Yes, Imma, she does. In fact, it was she who broached the subject a year ago. Since then I have thought of nothing else."

I was deeply offended. "Broached the subject? To *you?!* It is not fitting! This is something that *parents* decide, not *children!*"

"Imma, things are done differently here. Sarah asked me first because she knew how you would react. Of course she intended to speak to you soon, but she thought you needed more time to get used to the idea."

I bit my lip. "I told her I had plans for you and

Evyatar. Why didn't she say something then?"

"Because she knew you would be angry and it might spoil things."

I sighed. It was true. I was impulsive where Sarah was restrained and weighed things in her mind before she spoke.

"Sarah will know how to handle Djeddi," Ruchama said confidently.

Because I still felt unhappy at what I deemed to be Sarah's treachery, I declined to get involved. I didn't even ask Ruchama what had been the outcome when she came back from the Bak-Levy household, but I soon guessed when Djeddi confronted me with a remarkable statement the next morning.

"Mazal," he inquired, "can you manage without me today in the shop?"

"Of course, Abba. You are not ill, Heaven forbid?" I asked, suddenly concerned.

"No, no – nothing like that. On my way home from the *Kotel* this morning, I met your nice young neighbor, Menachem. He wants to take me on a *tiyul* today to see the *beit knesset* his family built. Perhaps it will be interesting. In any event, I did not wish to offend him."

I busied myself at the stove, ignoring the look of delight on Ruchama's face. They were gone for several hours and I was busy with customers when Djeddi returned. As he entered the shop, he nodded to me and took his customary place on the low stool in the workroom, wordlessly busying himself with his craft. It was late afternoon, closing time, before I had a chance to talk to him.

"Did you enjoy the *tiyul*," I asked apprehensively.

"It was most interesting. Did you know, daughter,

they call Tiferet Yisrael the Nisan Bak synagogue, after
Menachem's grandfather? Before half a century, he raised
funds and designed a proper house of prayer for the
Ashkenazi Chasidim It was to the Emperor of Austria
that he had to turn for permission to build it, and the
Almighty softened the Emperor's heart. Permission was
granted but thirteen more years passed before the project
was begun. A very great donation came from his father,
Rabbi Yisrael, may his memory be a blessing. He was
the founder of the Ruzhin-Sadigora dynasty, I think it is
called, and holy spiritual leader of the Chasidim here in
the Holy Land. He was a man of such influence that the
ruler of Russia, Nikolai I, had thrown him out of his
country. It seems Czar Nikolai was very, very angry when
he heard about Rav Yisrael's donation; he had wanted
that same plot to build on it a Greek Orthodox church."

It was unlike Djeddi to talk so much, but he went on
almost without drawing a breath, his face animated. I had
always known him to be wise and learned, but uneducated
in the ways of the world. Perhaps I had underestimated
him. "The next thing that happened," he continued, "was
that they uncovered there a tomb of a Moslem sheikh,
and they had to bargain at length with the Kadi until he
agreed to allow the remains of their holy sheikh to be
reinterred outside the city walls. And then there were more
extortion attempts by one Arab resident who claimed that
the sheikh had appeared to him in a dream and complained
about the desecration of his grave for building a
synagogue. Well, the Arabs went mad over this, as you
and I both know only they can, until the Kadi changed
his mind. Still, he had given his word to Nisan Bak. So in
his next Friday sermon at El Aqsa mosque, he pretended
that the sheikh had come also to him in a dream, and do
you know what he said?"

By this time, I too was also caught up in the tale. I sat next to my father who went on with his recitation almost as though he were alone. "The Kadi told them: 'Allah's beloved, Ibrahim, summoned me in Paradise protesting: *Why do the sons of your nations deny from the sons of my nation the building of a house of worship? Are we not brothers?* Verily, I promised our father Ibrahim to intercede for him and now I beg my sons to help rather than hinder this pious work so that I may rest in peace...' What do you think of that for a shrewd Arab?"

"So there were no more difficulties?" I asked.

"Unfortunately there were. To get a building permit from the Sublime Porte was very hard. A man called Count Pizzamano, or some such, who was the Austrian consul, tried to help but still it took years. Kaiser Franz Josef of Austria interceded in Constantinople. Finally, the *firman* was issued. So much trouble, Mazal, for a Jew to gain the permission of the gentiles to build a house of worship. May the Almighty grant us sovereignty over our Land, so that we never again will have to beg the mercy of the *goyim!"*

"Amen!" I said with feeling. I was just as intrigued with the story as he was, so I waited expectantly for him to continue. He took a long swallow of *gisher,* and then went on.

"The permit said they may build a structure so many ells long, so many ells wide, and so many ells high with two stones But they needed much more money and Nisan Bak was in despair: if they sent emissaries to richer lands across the seas to raise the funds, the journeying would use half of the donations. And they could not delay the building in case the authorities changed their minds again.

"So how long did it take?"

"Fourteen years," my father replied, shaking his

head. "Do not forget that they were building also the Churvah synagogue of Rav Yehudah He-Chasid. The *kehillah* was growing and more space was needed. Do you know, Mazal, who gave the biggest donation to this Ashkenazi synagogue?"

I shook my head.

"A Sephardi Jew!" he said wonderingly. "His name was Yechezkel Sassoon of Calcutta – he gave 14,000 rupees. And yet another donor was a gentile of the highest eminence, the Emperor Franz Josef himself." I had always loved hearing stories and now I felt I was again the child listening to her father, the young wife listening to Ezra.

"It is amazing, Mazal, how this came about. The Almighty works in wondrous ways and often chooses *shelichim* we would never imagine to carry out His plans. The Emperor was on his way to the ceremony of opening the Canal of Suez and he stopped to visit Jerusalem. He asked about the synagogue about which he had spoken with the Sultan. But when he saw the unfinished building, he felt he had been deceived and demanded that the architect Nisan Bak be brought before him. 'Where did you study?' he asked, and Nisan Bak replied, 'At a private college, your Majesty.' The Emperor said: 'Did they not teach you there that a building needs a roof?' and Nisan Bak answered: 'It has been removed – just as your subjects doff their hats – in deference to your Imperial presence.'"

"The Kaiser must have been furious at such insolence!" I said.

"So one would think, Mazal, but no. He was amused. 'I hope it will soon be replaced,' he said and gave Bak a gift of 1,000 francs." The synagogue was dedicated three years later. Altogether, it took twenty-nine years.

"It is a very unusual building," Djeddi continued. "It has a flat square roof beneath its dome. 'The Glory of

Israel' – it is a very fitting name, even though everyone calls it Nisan Bak synagogue. The boy Menachem is very proud of his ancestry, and rightly so. It is good to see such respect for grandparents and great-grandparents in the youth of today."

I swallowed hard. The time had come. "Do you like Menachem?" I asked, trying to keep my tone casual.

"I just said so, did I not?"

"Ruchama likes him too," I ventured.

Djeddi frowned. "We must get her married. She must not have such thoughts. We will go to Kfar Shiloach and talk to Yifat and Reuven about their son. I told you years ago she should be married, but you were stubborn. You wanted her to finish school. The sooner we arrange the Chinah, the better!"

"Things are different here, Abba," I said. "Girls are educated too. And from what I have seen, it is not bad."

"It can be, if it leads their thoughts in wrong directions. Did you not love the husband we chose for you?"

"Of course I did." Tears sprang to my eyes at the memory of Ezra. "But I knew no other boys. Ruchama has grown up with all of Sarah's children, and always very properly. Menachem has been like a brother to her since she was an infant, but once they were grown they never spent time alone together. You know they are both very stringent about such things, just as they were raised to be."

"He is not her brother," Djeddi said severely. "He is not Yemenite. You are making me angry. Why must we speak of this?"

I started to cry. "Ruchama wants to marry him. His parents agree. And she will consider no other."

Djeddi rose and began to pace around the kitchen.

"It is because of your sister that this has happened," he said bitterly. "I should have prevented her marriage and Ruchama would know that such a thing in our family is not permitted."

"You could not have prevented it, Abba. She was in Eretz Yisrael and you were in Sana'a. By the time you came, she was a mother."

"But now I am here. I can prevent this, and I *will*. Send Ruchama to me."

I went to get her, but when I found her, she was crying. And it had nothing to do with her grandfather's opposition to her marriage.

17

RUCHAMA HAD A CRUMPLED SLIP of paper in her hand. When I found her in Djeddi's room behind the workshop, she was in a state of great agitation, folding this paper and then smoothing it out again on the desk.

"What is it, my dear?" I cried out. Seeing her tear-stained face, all thoughts of the conversation with my father suddenly vanished.

"It's from Shalom!" she blurted out. "He's run away, Imma! This note was just delivered to me." I had seen Pinchas, one of Shalom's less reputable friends, come into the shop a little earlier and ask to see Ruchama, but I had taken little notice, so immersed was I in the discussion with my father.

My heart pounded. I didn't think I could survive so much buffeting in one day. "What do you mean, run away? Where has he gone? What does he say?"

She read his words slowly, and I vaguely wondered why she was squinting over the writing which looked quite clear.

Dear Ruchama, I have had enough. School is not for me; the workshop is not for me. I know that I will just keep disappointing Djeddi and Imma. I am not like Assaf and I never will be. I am going away to work for a while, with some friends. I am going to Beit Lechem, where

I understand there is plenty of building work to be had. Tell Imma not to come after me – it is dangerous there for a Jewish woman. I feel stifled at home. I want to try living in a different way. But I will miss you, Ruchama. Take care.

Shalom

It was ironic that the letter was more neatly written than any of the school work he had ever handed in. "What shall we do?" Ruchama wailed. "Beit Lechem is no place for my brother – a place of mosques and churches and highwaymen!"

"He is so young," I mourned. "He is still a baby. What will become of him?!"

By this time, because I had not returned to the workshop, Djeddi came to seek me out. He was not surprised to find Ruchama there, crying.

"You told her I will not allow her marriage?" he asked.

"No, no, Abba. Not yet. Something more important has come up."

He regarded me as though I were mad. "Something more important than your only daughter's marriage?"

I nodded. "Yes, Abba. Sit down. Shalom has run away!"

I waited for an explosion, but none came. My father gave a deep sigh and shook his head. "It was to be expected," he said sadly. "It was like trying to contain a raging fire in a small grate. Shalom needs to be free. We tried to make him a scholar, but it could never be. He has not the patience for learning. We tried to teach him the trade, but he is not interested in the delicate work of silversmithing. He needs to use his muscles – he is but a boy and already he has strong shoulders, strong arms, and he is fleet-footed too. He has a wild spirit. We cannot curb it but we should have sought ways to direct it."

"Where did it come from?" Ruchama asked piteously. "Not from you, Djeddi, not from our parents."

"Perhaps from my brother," Djeddi reflected. "Itamar could have been a silversmith too – the Turks would have respected him more. But he would laugh at me, stooped over, hammering out silver filigree all day. So he worked at the stone quarry, doing heavy, back-breaking work for the Turkish masters who treated him worse than their animals.

I knew that my Uncle Itamar was dead. I didn't want to know how, so filled with dread was my heart for my younger son.

"We have to bring him home!" Ruchama sobbed.

"No, child, we cannot do that," Djeddi said. "He will only run away again. We must find a way for him to want to come back again. He must know that we will accept him as he is, not as we wish him to be."

We were all quiet, thinking what could be done. Ruchama wanted to send Assaf after him to bring him back, but I agreed with Djeddi that it would be futile. Shalom must always have smarted under the comparison to his scholarly brother, and although I had never done so intentionally, I was doubtless to blame by continually holding up Assaf as an example. I was tortured by feelings of guilt.

Beit Lechem was a full day's ride from Jerusalem by carriage. The Pasha had made his first attempt at road-making on this route, a project, I was told, that had been under way for almost forty years. The paving had been spasmodic, depending on how much money was in his exchequer. Some parts of the road were fully paved, many others more rough and impassable. Some sections had not yet known the mattock or the spade and were barely discernible. There was also the danger of attack by bandits all along the route, a major cause for worry although Shalom had no valuables and would have been regarded by them as an unlikely target.

"We could ask Sarah what to do," Ruchama finally ventured.

"This is family business!" I said sharply. "Not everyone has to know it. And stop rubbing your eyes."

"Imma, they hurt me," she replied. "They feel so dry and I don't see very clearly."

My irritation with her disappeared, and was replaced by concern. "Why have you not said something before?"

"So much has been happening. I was too involved with working out a plan to tell you about Menachem."

"It will not do, Ruchama," Djeddi interjected. "You cannot marry that Ashkenazi young man."

Everything was suddenly too much for me...the collapse of my dreams for Ruchama to marry Evyatar; my young son running away to Beit Lechem; and now my daughter having trouble with her eyes. I no longer felt like the successful, independent woman Sarah always told me I had become. Instead I felt vulnerable and helpless. I had made money and bought property, but what good were possessions when my life was in tatters?

Djeddi was examining Ruchama's eyes. "They look a bit strange," he commented. "There seems to be a film over them."

Ruchama nodded. "It is hard for me to be in the sunlight, Djeddi. Strong light hurts me."

"You have herbs for this, Mazal?" asked my father.

I felt so weary, I could barely answer. "I don't rely on them anymore, Abba. I will summon Dr. Wallach."

"Are you also not well, daughter?" my father asked, suddenly aware of my slumped shoulders and look of despair.

I didn't answer. I was a woman of thirty-three, but I felt old and weak.

As if catching my thoughts, Djeddi murmured: "I lift up my eyes to the hills, whence my help will come. My help comes from the Lord..." After a pause, he continued: "We must go to the *Kotel,* my daughter, and pray. First we consult the Divine Physician, then we will call your Dr. Wallach."

I nodded. I could barely drag my feet but I grabbed a shawl and followed my father. "You stay here," was Djeddi's parting remark to Ruchama. "Rest and close your eyes. And do not go to the Chosh, to the neighbor's!"

This was one more barb of pain. If Djeddi could not be persuaded to permit Ruchama to marry Menachem, what would this do to our friendship with the Bak-Levy family? How could I continue to live next to them? And bereft of Sarah's friendship, what would my life be? She had always been a mother-figure to me, an anchor in a turbulent sea of despair, a calm source of wisdom.

As I followed my father through cobbled alleys to the Western Wall, I felt as though I carried the whole weight of the world on my shoulders. That world, and my life, were falling apart and I had no strength left to fight.

18

THE KOTEL HA-MA'ARAVI
was a towering presence in the sunset.
The shadows were lengthening when we
arrived, deep purple changing to inky black, and
the sky became filled with glittering stars, like
diamonds scattered on a length of blue velvet. The sight
made me painfully aware of our insignificance within
the vastness of the universe. Would the Almighty hear
my small voice?

Only a tiny section of the Wall remained intact and
exposed – our holiest site, the last remnant of the great
Temple which the Romans had destroyed. The Ottoman
rulers allowed us to pray there, but they did not make it
easy. We still could bring no chairs, nor erect a *mechitzah*
to separate the men from the women as we prayed.
Usually I came there to recite *Tehillim* for the end of our
exile, at this Wailing Wall where there was always the
real sound of wailing for the losses sustained by our
People over the last 2,000 years, and the sight of it never
ceased to fill me with awe.

Jerusalem had been conquered countless times, and
whether the rulers had been Persian, Egyptian, Seleucid,
Greek, Roman or Turkish, they had all oppressed us and
made our lives bitter. In some ways the Ottomans were
less cruel than their predecessors, but still we suffered.
They did nothing to protect us from the Arabs who defiled
our prayers at the Wall by throwing buckets of dirty water
down on us, despite the extra rows of stones that had
been added. They often galloped through the narrow

passageway on horseback, forcing us to huddle against the Wall to avoid being trampled underfoot. Yet we felt safe there, because we knew that the *Shechinah,* the Divine Presence, had never departed, and whatever we prayed for in that sacred spot would ultimately be granted us.

My prayers that night were not selfless ones for my people, but just for my family. I rested my hot face against the cool, timeless stones. Before I closed my eyes, I saw my father at the other end, praying with the men, the long robes which he still wore swaying to the motion of his body as he rocked back and forth, no doubt entreating the Almighty for the same merciful intervention as I did.

As always at this holy place, I soon lost all awareness of my surroundings. The texture of the rock against my face was comforting, and I also rested the palms of my hands on it. At first no words came, but soon, as the tears poured down my cheeks a torrent of words began to flow unchecked, about my daughter's future happiness as a wife, a cure for her eye affliction, and a prayer for the safety of my younger son.

I didn't know how to ask for specific things...whether it would be better for Ruchama to marry Menachem or Evyatar. Instead I prayed that her marriage would be a happy and fulfilling union. I was terrified about her eyes because very many Jews in Eretz Yisrael, especially those from Eastern countries, were afflicted with a dreaded eye disease and many had lost their sight, may this not be Ruchama's fate! Shalom – I felt I had failed him. He needed something that neither I nor his grandfather had been able to give him. It was because of our failure that he preferred to work at back-breaking labor with rough companions than to live in comfort and security with his family, in an atmosphere of Torah and *mitzvot.*

I had lost all sense of time. When I finally opened my eyes, I saw Djeddi standing at a distance waiting for me. Everyone else had departed – it was not safe to be at the Wall late at night, nor to traverse the feebly-lit narrow alleys. But I had no sense of danger as we walked to my home in the Chosh, only an enormous sense of relief. I had poured out my feelings of weakness and inadequacy, and now the Almighty would take over the burden that had become too heavy for my frail shoulders.

Djeddi usually came to eat with us in the evenings, and I always prepared the traditional food he enjoyed. Ruchama, having wearied of waiting for us at the shop, had preceded us home. Despite the turmoil she was undergoing, she had prepared a Yemenite meal for us, doubtless in part to win her grandfather's favor; she herself preferred the more bland Ashkenazi food. A pot of *shaweeya* – spicy meatballs with squash – was simmering on the stove and she had even baked *saluf,* our traditional pita bread. Djeddi patted her hand as a sign of approval as he passed her, but did not speak. Assaf, who normally ate at his yeshivah, was already sitting at the table looking very somber and it was easy to guess that Ruchama had summoned him and told him about Shalom.

Although none of us had much appetite, we wanted to show our appreciation of Ruchama's efforts so we toyed with our food and somehow got through the meal. I kept stealing glances at Ruchama whose eyes looked strange to me, the lids appearing almost to turn inwards. Catching my scrutiny, she ventured: "I made some eye pads, Imma, from a mixture of distilled herbs. I think it has helped." I nodded, no longer having any faith in them but knowing that she did.

"I used the ground dried lady's mantle and the dried

fennel and poured boiling water over them," she continued. "I let it steep for ten minutes, as you showed me, and then I strained the liquid and soaked two pads that I made from pieces of lint. It felt very soothing on my eyes."

I shrugged. "Soothing isn't curing."

Djeddi frowned at me. "Why do you speak this way, Mazal? Your mother kept us healthy with only herbs. We never had a doctor."

"My mother is dead," I said bitterly, "and my husband is dead. My daughter will see a *doctor.*" There was silence, each of us busy with our own thoughts.

Finally, Assaf, who had sat through the meal looking pale and tense, made the first reference to the pain we were all feeling at seeing Shalom's empty chair. "I want to go to Beit Lechem and talk to Shalom. Maybe I can convince him to come home."

I shook my head. "Thank you, my son, but he would never listen to you."

"I'm his older brother. Since we have no father, it's my responsibility."

"You are a good boy," Djeddi said, "perhaps too good to be able to convince your brother of anything."

"I don't understand. Are you saying he left because of me?"

Djeddi chose his words carefully. "Yes, in a way. You are everything that Shalom knew he could never be. You are a scholar, you are pious, a credit to your family and your teachers. Rather than be second-rate, he chose not to try at all."

"Second-rate! To me he is the best: he's witty, has many friends, and always has an answer for everything. I love him," he confessed brokenly, "but I never let him know it. I always criticized him and tried to push him to do things my way, even when it was clear that he could not. I let him down."

"We all did," I commented sadly.

"Not Ruchama," Assaf said. "She always listened to him."

Djeddi nodded. "What do you suggest we do, granddaughter?" he asked her. I knew what an effort the question took. Old traditions die hard and it was unheard of for a man, the elder of our family, to ask advice from a woman – in this case, a young inexperienced girl.

"I think we should do nothing yet," she answered quietly. "I've been thinking it over all afternoon long. If we chase after him to bring him home, again we'll make him feel like a naughty child and shame him before his friends. Why not let him find a job there, at least for a while, so that he can earn some money and feel like a man who has been a success at something. It will be an achievement for him, to go to a dangerous place like Beit Lechem, and succeed – even in a small way – in doing something none of us would be brave enough to attempt. He has to come home when he is ready... I don't think it will take too long."

"You are a wise child," said Djeddi quietly. Ruchama's words proved to be prophetic, although I would have preferred it to be a different reason that brought Shalom back to the arms of his family.

19

DR. MOSHE WALLACH, STILL A young man in his mid-thirties, had become a household name in the Old City since his arrival eight years earlier. The hospital he had been hired to direct was still two years away from completion, although permission to construct it had long ago been given. The Turks were afraid that a modern medical facility would generate increased Jewish immigration, so the property was at first registered privately in the names of Rabbi Shelomo Levin and Yehoshua Moshe Schlank, two Jerusalemites, and while construction progressed, Dr. Wallach continued his work in the Old City.

Everyone knew him to be a very religious and compassionate man and often his prescriptions might be not for medication, but for milk for undernourished children, or meat for an adult suffering from malnutrition. Even when he closed his clinic at the end of the day, his work was not finished; at night he made the rounds to the poor in their homes and brought them the medication that he knew they could not afford to buy.

I was in a different category: I could afford to pay. But when I took Ruchama to the clinic the next morning, we still had to stand in line behind dozens of very sick patients. Malaria, diphtheria and cholera were all widespread at the time, and it was only through the Almighty's mercy that we had been spared until now. I was distressed to see a number of people with eye symptoms similar to Ruchama's. Although many of those waiting obviously had no money to pay for treatment, each one was received as courteously and compassionately as we were when eventually, after several hours, we reached the head of the line.

Dr. Wallach did not even ask me what the problem was: he saw all the symptoms as soon as he looked at my daughter. "Trachoma – another one!" he said, shaking his head wearily. "Where did you come from?"

"Our home is in the Chosh," I answered.

The young doctor smiled. "I mean from what country. Yemen?"

I nodded.

"The situation is very bad," he said. "Do you know there are thousands of cases in the country of this eye disease just now?"

"Will I be blind?" Ruchama asked in a frightened voice.

"I don't know," he replied gently." I have no miracle cure. I think I should send you to the British Ophthalmic Hospital, on the road to Bethlehem. I hear they do good work."

"Is it a church hospital?" I asked.

"It was founded by the Order of St. John."

"Then I don't want my daughter to go there," I said stubbornly. All the tales I had heard of missionaries converting Jews under the pretext of offering medical help, rang in my ears.

"I am not an ophthalmologist," Dr. Wallach said. "The specialists at St. John's know more about this affliction than I do." I remained adamant.

"Do you know how serious this condition is?" he asked us.

"Please tell me about it," Ruchama begged, tears coursing down her cheeks.

"It is the greatest single worldwide cause of progressive loss of vision," the doctor explained. "Chlamydia trachomatis. You have all the symptoms – pale nodules on the lining of the lids, a hazy film over the cornea. Fortunately your case has not progressed far, but I can't promise anything."

"Please try to help my daughter!" I begged him. "I will pay whatever the cost. I have money.

For the first time, his weariness was replaced by anger. "Madam, do you think if you had no money, I wouldn't try?"

"I'm sorry," I apologized. "I meant no offense. It's just that I don't want you to spare any expense, no matter what the medication or treatment costs. I can afford it – even if you must bring some rare medicine from another country."

Dr. Wallach nodded. He walked to his small dispensary and began preparing some drops and a solution. When he spoke to Ruchama, his voice was again gentle and compassionate. "You will apply these drops twice every day. They will help soothe the eyes and prevent adhesion of the lids due to conjunctivitis."

Ruchama began to tell him of the herbal infusion she had made, and I held my breath, fearing he would ridicule such an old-fashioned remedy. But I was wrong. "That is very good," he said. "There is no harm in using that as well. However, I have heard from the eye doctors at St. John's that they are having some success with an application of sulfonamides that are taken orally, so let us try that too." He handed Ruchama a second bottle.

I was surprised to hear that a man like Dr. Wallach, with his neatly-trimmed beard and high black *kippah,* would have contact with gentile physicians. "You are not afraid to consult them?" I ventured.

He smiled. "Men of medicine learn from one another. We speak as colleagues. In His wisdom, the Almighty imparted knowledge of science to Jew and gentile, and often we must share that knowledge in order to serve His creatures. When I treat an Arab patient, it is of no moment to me that he is Moslem – he is a human being, created in God's image, and he is in need of medical help. I am but His humble emissary."

I had my doubts about the wisdom of associating with gentiles, but I realized he thought my fears rather childish and naive. Still, Dr. Wallach was a relative newcomer to Jerusalem and was not aware of all the cases of Jews who had fallen victim to the missionaries after accepting their favors. But this was neither the time nor the place for such a discussion.

"You must come to me again every week," he told Ruchama. "If it is hard for you to find your way here, send a message and I will visit you at home."

I was wracked with fear. "Will her condition become so bad that she won't be able to see?"

"It is possible," he replied gravely. "It is a very virulent disease and there are many cases which have proved incurable."

We walked home in silence. I wanted to grip Ruchama's arm, to hold her close, but I knew it would only deepen her despair. All my dreams for my beautiful, talented daughter were dissipating. She was my first-born and her pain was my pain. If her father had lived, we could have shared the sorrow and comforted each other. Instead I grieved alone.

"If it could be me in your place, I would accept it gladly," I finally told her as we reached our house. She nodded and squeezed my hand, but didn't answer.

We heard the sound of voices as we mounted the

stairs, and going inside, I was surprised to see Yifat and Reuven talking to Assaf, who was still at home. It was not the day for her to bring her embroidery and in any case, she usually delivered it to the shop. I did not feel like entertaining visitors, even such dear friends, but I hastened to offer them refreshments. Ruchama left the room and Assaf joined her.

Seeing my confusion, Yifat said quietly: "We came for a special reason, Mazal. Please come and sit down. Assaf has already given us something to drink."

Gratefully I sank into a chair. I had no strength left in my body to do anything that required initiative – I think at that moment I would have obeyed anyone. My instincts told me that it had to be bad news. It was inconceivable that, the way my life was going, the tidings could be good.

"It is about our son Evyatar." Reuven took up the narrative when he saw that his wife was embarrassed to continue. "There is no easy way to say this, Mazal, but Evyatar doesn't want to marry Ruchama."

I grimaced. It was almost funny because soon I would have had to tell them that Ruchama didn't want to marry their son. Bitterly I wondered how they had learned of her eye affliction so quickly. However, Yifat's next words reassured me that they knew nothing about it.

"She is a beautiful girl," Yifat hastily added, "and we care for her as a daughter. But she is..." – she hesitated, averting her eyes before she went on – "...strange. She is so quiet and withdrawn, and that doesn't appeal to Evyatar."

I nodded mutely. It should have been a relief to me that I had been spared the unpleasant job of telling them the same story in reverse, but the only emotion I felt was an all-encompassing desolation.

"Evyatar has met someone," his father continued

relentlessly. "She is also from Sana'a, and she has come to live with her family in Kfar Shiloach. She is more in the tradition of our people – a wonderful housekeeper and also a very good weaver. Already she helps Yifat with the embroidery."

"It's not necessary to explain," I interrupted him. "I understand what you are saying. It is for the best."

Relief flooded Yifat's features. "You are not angry?"

I shook my head. "No, I am not angry." I guessed that Yifat was also worried that the revelation might mean the end of her livelihood. "Now that you have two pairs of hands, you will be able to bring me more of your work – it is very popular."

Impulsively she came over and kissed me. "Thank you," she whispered. "Thank you, my dear friend."

I clasped her hand. I truly loved Yifat, my lifelong friend, and although I had begun offering her work for sale in my store out of a wish to help her, I spoke the truth when I said it had become popular. Tourists who came to buy our jewelry were also delighted to take back with them some of her delicate scrolled embroidery as an example of craftmanship they would never see in their own countries.

After they left, Ruchama came back downstairs. She had overheard most of the conversation. "Don't be upset, Imma, that your plans for me have not worked out. What they said is true. I *am* a bit strange."

"You are not!" I cried out. "You're just very sensitive. It's a kind of..." I searched for the word.

"Refinement?" she interjected. "Perhaps, but you must realize I would not have made Evyatar happy, even though you wanted it so much. It would have been different with Menachem."

Chapter Nineteen

I felt myself go pale. "What do you mean *'would have been'?*"

"I cannot marry anyone," she said, her voice hopeless. "I may be blind very soon. Dr. Wallach is not sure if he can cure me. Perhaps that is why God gave me talent to paint. I already have captured the beauty of His creation in many of my sketches. At least I have those."

I couldn't speak. Ever since she was born, Ruchama had loved nature: the sky at dawn and at sunset, a clump of wildflowers, trees putting on new green lace in the spring... These had filled my daughter's heart with joy. There could be no more dreadful affliction for her than the loss of her sight.

"Ruchama, please, please don't give up hope!" I implored.

"No, I won't do that. But while I am hoping and waiting to be cured, I don't expect Menachem to wait for me. It may be a long time before I am well; it may be never."

I watched her go up the stairs to her room. Her back was erect, her thick braid a gleaming black rope against the pale blue of her dress. My heart was leaden with pain.

20

WITH ALL OF MY FAMILY
WORRIES, it was lucky that I had my
work at the store to keep me busy and distract
me. Although Djeddi did most of the jewelry-
making now, as he was more skilled than I was, I still
liked to make some pieces just to keep my hand in.
Tourists were fascinated by the whole process, particularly
by our delicate filigree and granulation work, and many
asked to peek in at Djeddi in the workshop. I realized
their curiosity was worth exploiting. I expected him to
refuse, but my father always surprised me.

"We are getting very busy, Abba," I remarked one
evening as we were closing up. "I think we should enlarge
the store – maybe open the workshop as part of the shop."

"And where would I work?" he asked mildly.

"That's the point. The customers want to *see* you.
They admire your jewelry so much and are interested in
how it's made. If you wouldn't object, I thought perhaps
we could make a sort of attraction. It would draw locals
as well as the tourist trade."

"Like a torch-juggling Arab in a traveling circus,
you mean?"

"Oh, no!" I said horrified. "I mean...

He laughed. "I am teasing you, Mazal. If you think
it will be good for business, than I will gladly juggle
torches or act like a monkey in a cage. We might have
need of much money for Ruchama, if it is the Merciful
One's will..." He did not finish the sentence, but I knew
that he meant if she became blind.

"Don't worry, Abba. *Baruch Hashem*, we are doing very well, financially," I assured him. "Your coming to Jerusalem and working with me has increased our profits beyond my dreams."

"That is very good. The Almighty strikes us with one hand and embraces us with the other. But now that we have seen how well *our* partnership works, we should take *another* partner."

"What do you mean?"

"Mazal, we must never forget those less fortunate. Yifat has contributed to our success, so why not make her a partner also? Instead of only selling us her embroidery, she should have a share now. Jerusalem is not like Sana'a, you know, where women only stayed in the kitchen and tended the little ones. Yifat has many mouths to feed – and her son's wedding," he added ruefully, remembering that Evyatar would not be marrying his granddaughter. "Your mother would have been happy to see it. She had a big heart and always gave *tzedakah* to the needy, even when we had little for ourselves."

I smiled at him, my heart filled with love. If I had made something of my life, much of it was due to the lessons and values instilled in me by my virtuous parents. I was overjoyed that Djeddi had agreed to my plan, knowing what an exotic note he would introduce to the store in his flowing robes, his turban head-dress and his untamed beard. "It is a very good idea, Abba. Yifat and Reuven are like our own family – if we progress, then their lives should also be easier."

"What shall we call the place?" he asked suddenly.

"What do you mean?"

"It must have a name, and a big sign, too. Ruchama must paint us a wooden sign to hang outside with a picture...I know – a *gargush!*" he said excitedly.

I looked at him in amazement. I still thought of my father as living in the eighteenth century, and here he was coming out with such a modern suggestion. A *gargush*, made of brocade or cotton, is worn by Jewish women of Yemen on their bridal day. It is a hood that encloses the head and neck completely, revealing just the middle of the unveiled face, and the borders of it are decorated with strands of silver chains and braided cords of silk and silver thread. Indeed, the image was ideal.

"Perhaps we can call the store 'Gargush'?" Djeddi suggested.

I was pensive, my mind returning to my beloved husband Ezra, who had taught me the craft of silversmithing and enabled me to support our children after his death. My hand automatically went to my throat, to the necklace he had given me on my wedding day.

"We will call it *The Pomegranate Pendant,*" I said resolutely. Our eyes met, glittering with unshed tears.

I was not sure that painting would be good for Ruchama's failing eyesight, but Djeddi told her his idea and it appealed to her; she too needed to be distracted from her worries.

The next morning Ruchama came to the shop to begin a sketch under Djeddi's direction, and said she would also serve any customers who came in while I was gone. However, the first person to enter the shop was not a customer – it was Menachem Bak-Levy.

Djeddi was in the adjoining workroom, and could not help but overhear the entire conversation. He related it to me later, when I returned from my rounds:

"My mother told me you wanted to speak to me," Menachem had said.

"Yes, Menachem," Ruchama began hesitantly. Then

she blurted out the whole sad, painful tale. "I have trachoma. I may soon go blind. Menachem, I want to release you from your vow to marry me."

"But I don't want to be released."

"I can't marry anyone – not now, maybe never."

"There is no one else for me, Ruchama. If I don't marry you, I will remain a bachelor until my dying day."

Her voice broke. "The first of all the commandments is to be fruitful and multiply. It would be a sin for you not to marry."

"I will marry," he replied gently. "I will marry you. We can be married whenever you wish – even now. If you lose your sight, I will care for you.

"No!" Ruchama said adamantly. "I will not be a burden to you. You are young, very pleasing to look on, and an outstanding scholar. Why should you not have the best?"

Seeing Djeddi standing in the doorway, Menachem appealed to him. "Please explain to your granddaughter that for me, with or without sight, she is not just the best, but the only woman I will consider for my wife. She is my *zivig,* the other half of my soul who was created for me in Heaven."

Djeddi stepped into the shop. "Do you mean what you are saying? That you want to marry my granddaughter even if she loses her sight and you must do everything for her?"

"I mean it," Menachem replied, "with all my heart."

Ruchama shook her head. "I will only marry you if I can see – if I can be cured. I will not change my mind."

Djeddi motioned Menachem into the workshop and closed the door between the two rooms. He held his hand out to him. "I bless you, my son," he said. "I was wrong. You are not Yemenite, but you have the heart of a

Yemenite. We have the same belief, only we say *zivug.* If you feel that Ruchama is your *zivug,* then you have my blessing. You have a fine name – Bak-Levy. What does 'Bak' come from?"

"It is an acronym for *b'nai Kedoshim,* descendants of the Sacred Ones."

Djeddi nodded. "It is a fitting name. Be patient, my son. Ruchama's affliction is very bitter, especially for an artist. She still has sight, but it is failing and Dr. Wallach makes no promises to cure her. But, with the Merciful One's help, she will be healed. If you are willing to wait, then it will help her through these dark days. She will have a good dowry..." he added.

"That is no concern of mine," Menachem replied. "Even if she were penniless, I would want to marry only her. I am a trained *sofer.* I can support her. I am now writing a *sefer Torah* for the Churvah synagogue. In addition to being a great honor, it will bring me a handsome sum of money. Ruchama will have everything she needs, when she is my wife."

"I think it will be good, Mazal," Djeddi said as he concluded his report. He turned back to the worktable to continue crafting an amber necklace, much favored by Moslems and our Turkish masters as gifts for their brides. Djeddi looked up and smiled at me. "That Menachem, he thinks like a Yemenite!" He was silent for a moment, and then, to my amazement, he added: "I did well to choose him as a husband for my granddaughter!"

Djeddi's turnabout might have been more amusing to witness if I could have shared his confidence that things would work out. I glanced at Ruchama, who was outside the shop sketching the new sign on a large shingle Djeddi had found. Her face was bent close to her work, her eyes squinting in the sunlight. My heart ached for her.

21

WHEN WEEK AFTER week passed with no sign of improvement in Ruchama's condition, I redoubled my efforts to perform acts of *chesed* in the hope that the Merciful One would bestow His *chesed* upon her. I visited the sick and increased my charity to the poor; I gave food to widows and orphans and dowries to impoverished brides. I felt almost driven, anxious to secure Divine Intervention. Djeddi did as well, and spent a great deal of time in the *beit knesset*. One morning when he returned from services, he had a stricken look.

"Are you feeling unwell, Abba?" I asked, greatly concerned.

"I am well, daughter, praise God," he replied, "but I suddenly realized that you had not told me of Yifat's response to our offer of partnership. Did you perhaps forget to speak with her?"

I felt the blood drain from my face and for a moment I couldn't breathe. "Abba, Abba, what have I done!" I cried.

"Surely it is because of this that Ruchama continues to suffer! I was so preoccupied that after we discussed the matter I...I simply forgot. It slipped my mind. Oh, oh, poor Yifat...!"

"Now, now, Mazal, you mustn't berate yourself so. The matter will be quickly rectified. Take your shawl – we will go to see her now." I closed the shop and we set out on foot for Kfar Shiloach. With each step I felt myself growing calmer, knowing in my heart that the solution to our dilemma lay just beyond Yifat's door. The burden of troubles was soon to be lifted.

Yifat was indeed so happy to receive our offer that she shed buckets of joyful tears. I assured her that we were only doing what was fitting and right, as she had contributed so significantly to our success. She gave me a basket full of new pieces she and her daughter-in-law had completed. "I haven't had time all month to bring it over myself," she said, "what with the *chaggim* and the new baby." Her workmanship was as stunning as ever. I had no doubt I'd be able to sell it all quickly.

We embraced warmly and took our leave. "The partnership was Abba's idea," I told her and she bowed her head to Djeddi in profound gratitude.

"May the Almighty bless you and Reuven and your children," he said.

We walked along the dusty path with a spring in our step. "Do you remember *Mori* Saadyah from the old country, Abba?" I asked.

"Why, of course, daughter. Did he not make aliyah with you and Ezra?"

"Yes, Abba," I replied. "He and his wife and three children. They live here, in Shiloach, where *Mori* Saadyah can gaze at Har Ha-zeitim each dawn. It is his desire to be among the first minyan to greet the Redeemer when he comes to the Holy City. There is his house – the one with the huge fig tree." I pointed to a small, tidy structure up ahead.

"I must stop and visit," Djeddi said enthusiastically, as I had known he would. *Mori* Saadyah was closer in age to Djeddi than most members of Jerusalem's Yemenite community, and the two would have much to talk about.

Mori Saadyah also had a very special story to tell, but I revealed not a hint of it to my father, so as not to diminish his enjoyment of it. When we reached *Mori* Saadyah's gate I waved Djeddi along and headed back to the shop.

Not long after *Mori* Saadyah and his family had settled into Kfar Shiloach, his wife gave birth to their fourth child – a beautiful baby boy whom they named Zecharyah. It was a fitting name for the son of a man on whose very doorstep stands the tomb of the Prophet Zecharyah, the Prophet who foretold of the Redemption. Zecharyah was the last child to be born to *Mori* Saadyah – he and his wife were no longer young – and he grew to be a precocious and quite handsome little boy.

Mori Saadyah spent most of the year immersed in Torah study and in perfecting his observance of the mitzvot. He was famous for the annual *Simchat Beit Ha-shoevah* – the lively celebration commemorating the water-drawing ceremony from the time of the *Beit Ha-mikdash* – which he hosted in his beautifully decorated *sukkah* and which was attended by many Ashkenazi guests as well as the entire Yemenite community.

Mori Saadyah was not a well-to-do man, but he had managed to bring many lovely carpets and tapestries from Sana'a and these he used to adorn the walls and floor of his *sukkah*. He had also brought from Sana'a a huge shofar, a ram's horn with *five* loops, which he would sound at the *Simchat Beit Ha-shoevah* in the midst of all the dancing and singing.

That enormous old fig tree in his courtyard was his main source of income. It produced a very bountiful crop of unusually large, succulent figs which he would sell in the shuk. And Zecharyah, as a youngster, always accompanied him to the marketplace and manned the scales. It was here that *Mori* Saadyah's wondrous tale began.

Zecharyah, being a lively and quite adorable child, befriended all the stall owners in the shuk, Arab and Jew alike, and often ran off to play with their children. One day, he disappeared, and although many searched for him far and wide, he could not be found. Needless to say, his father was inconsolable.

Unbeknownst to anyone, Zecharyah had been kidnapped by a Moslem stall owner and taken to the man's home in el-Azariyah, to be a companion for his only son. In a short time, the little boy ceased to feel homesick and became convinced – as did the villagers of el-Azariyah – that he was a nephew of the stall owner who had come to stay. His Yemenite complexion and flawless Arabic made the falsehood entirely credible.

Months passed, and as Sukkot neared, *Mori* Saadyah felt he could not hold a *Simchat Beit Ha-shoevah* celebration as in the past. His heart was broken over the loss of his precious child. But the great *Chachamim* and *Rabbanim* – including Rav Yosef Chaim Sonnenfeld and Rav Mordechai Leib Rubin, the *Rav Av Beit Din* – urged him to set aside his pain and do as he had done each year. Reluctantly, he followed their instructions, and the celebration took place on the second day of *Chol Ha-moed.*

Naturally, all those who attended tried their utmost to gladden *Mori* Saadyah's heart and lift his spirits. The singing and dancing, therefore, were even more lively than in years gone by and the music carried across the slopes of the valley all the way to el-Azariyah. There, little Zecharyah, asleep in the stall owner's home, stirred. The forgotten yet familiar melodies, the rhythm of the tambour drum, the high-pitched notes of the *chalil,* and, finally, the blast of *Mori* Saadyah's fabulous shofar aroused a longing in his soul. He tiptoed out into the night and followed the music all the way home.

I was certain that *Mori* Saadyah's rendition of his miraculous tale would take a great deal longer to recite than my recollection had. Djeddi would surely be savoring it for hours yet. I glanced back at Kfar Shiloach from just outside the Ashpot Gate, pleased to note that the housing project there was nearing completion. Soon Yifat and Reuven would be able to move into a lovely, spacious home built with funds donated by Baron Maurice de Hirsch of Argentina and other generous philanthropists. And, with the Almighty's help, profits from *The Pomegranate Pendant* would enable them to be financially independent at last.

22

THE MONTH OF
MARCHESHVAN mirrored my mood
– an autumnal melancholy. Winter, it seemed,
had come early this year. The days grew shorter;
the leaves of the trees changed color, fell to the ground
in a dismal brown heap and were trampled underfoot.
The rain drizzled, clouds drifted across the sky like dirty
torn rags and we huddled into woolen cloaks when we
walked around Jerusalem. For Ruchama, the days had
become almost totally dark; she could see outlines, but
no clear images. There was only one real ray of light:
Shalom had come home.

He walked in one evening unannounced, just as we
were sitting down to supper in the Chosh, and everyone
rushed to greet him. Only Ruchama remained quietly
seated, unsure who he was. He motioned us to be still,
and sat down beside her.

"Ruchama, why didn't you tell me? Why didn't you
send me a message?"

Her face lit up. "Shalom?"

"I've come back to look after you until you are well.
I will be your eyes," he declared.

My eyes were full of tears, and even though it had
taken a tragedy to bring it about, I was filled with gratitude
that my youngest child had come home in time to be with
us for Chanukah. He was still a young boy, yet he had the
physique of a man from the hard, physical labor he must
have been doing and his hands were calloused and work-
roughened. But his voice when he spoke to his sister was

gentle.

I had wanted to let him know about Ruchama's failing eyesight but she had refused to allow it. "He will hear about it from someone soon enough," she had assured me. "I only want him to come home when he feels ready, when it is *his* decision," and of course she was right. Many months had passed, but eventually someone from Jerusalem had told him, and he had come to help his sister.

He didn't want to talk about the job he'd been doing in not Beit Lechem – we knew it was construction work of some kind – so we didn't persist. He was proud that he'd earned money, been independent for a while, and now felt like a man rather than the little boy who had left, continually scolded both at school and at home. Assaf was delighted to have his brother back and made a real effort to be a friend to him without preaching or moralizing.

But it was with Ruchama that Shalom excelled. We had always thought of him as rough and undisciplined, yet with his sister he was amazingly kind and sensitive. I would watch from the window as he guided her around the garden. She would turn her face to the early morning sun which still sometimes struggled through the clouds. "It feels so good, Shalom," she would tell him. Then she would bend down and touch a flower. "What is this one?"

Haltingly he would describe it to her. "Well, it's pink and the blossoms all kind of droop."

"A cyclamen!" she said in delight, her long artistic fingers tracing its surface. "Now I can feel the leaves. They're dark green, aren't they?"

Shalom would stare at the plant, trying to find something in his terms of reference to describe it for his sister. "They're not just one color. They're like copper pipe left out in the rain, sort of streaked with light green lines."

"How pretty it must be."

"Yes," Shalom would admit. "It's pretty. There's a butterfly on it now."

"Oh, tell me about it, Shalom."

"It's just a butterfly – two wings, you know...."

"I don't want to forget. I may never see a butterfly again, or a dewdrop nestling in the heart of a rose, or even a snail leaving a trail of silver on the garden path." And my daughter would begin to weep.

"Don't cry, Ruchama," Shalom would say awkwardly. "You'll get better, I'm sure of it. This butterfly, it's white and its wings are like that dress Imma wore on Shabbat..."

"Like velvet?"

"Yes, like velvet, soft and plushy."

Then Ruchama would laugh at him and they would move on to another plant, with Ruchama guessing its color and Shalom telling her she was right, even when she wasn't, just to see the delight on her face.

When we thought there was no chance of recovery, and Ruchama had refused even to let Menachem visit her, we received a message from Dr. Wallach, asking us to come to his clinic again. Ruchama did not want to admit her helplessness by asking him to come to our home, and the streets of the Old City were too narrow for a carriage to traverse, so we set out, Shalom and I, one on either side of her to guide her.

Dr. Wallach examined her closely. "There is no improvement from the weeks of treatment," he finally admitted. "The lining of the lids still has all these pale nodules and I see the lids themselves are inverting. Now, I do not wish to raise any false hopes, but I have found a remedy which has proved successful with some patients. However, I must warn you that it is quite drastic and may in fact do more harm than good."

"What is it?" I asked, my heart pounding.

"It is a powder made from bluestone – copper sulphate," he explained. "I would like to try it on Ruchama, but I am hesitant to do so."

"Doctor, I have nothing to lose," she pleaded. "I am already almost blind."

He looked at me. I nodded slowly. What choice was there?

We took the precious powder, afraid to place too much hope in it. "Continue with the other treatment too," Dr. Wallach advised her, "and follow the directions carefully. May the One Who Heals the Infirm be with you."

After a week, when Ruchama told me that she thought the new remedy was helping, I dismissed it as a product of her overworked imagination. However, a week after that, when I came home tired from the store, Ruchama was waiting for me with a smile on her face. "Imma, you are wearing a pink dress with a mauve headscarf, aren't you?"

I looked at her wearily. "Is this some kind of game?"

"No, it's not. Imma, I can see, even colors! The powder is working."

My hands were trembling as I turned her face towards the light. The nodules had disappeared from the lining of her eyelids and her eyes, although still a bit cloudy, had lost their film. "We must go to Dr. Wallach and show him," I cried, unable to contain my excitement.

"I've already been to the clinic," she replied. "Shalom took me. Dr. Wallach confirmed it – he said another week and my sight should be fully restored. Oh,

Imma, I am so happy!"

I embraced her, my heart overflowing with joy. Djeddi, who had witnessed the entire scene, was also overcome with emotion. "Praise be the Almighty Healer!" he exclaimed, tears of happiness trickling down his cheeks. "And now you will marry Menachem Bak-Levy?"

Ruchama nodded, smiling.

"A Chinah ceremony?" Djeddi asked hesitantly. "Although, perhaps..."

She didn't let him finish. "Of course, Djeddi. You said it yourself: Menachem has a Yemenite heart!"

It was not quite as my Chinah had been. It took place a week before the wedding. Ruchama wore the traditional costume, even the *gargush,* the bracelets, the jeweled breastplate, and the wide pants under the gold embroidered gown. With great love, I completed her outfit by fastening around her neck my own pomegranate pendant.

My dear friend Sarah and her husband and family smiled uncomfortably as they heard the women ululate, frightening away the evil spirits. They flinched a bit at the loud, throbbing music, and they only nibbled at the unfamiliar spicy food. But when I put the circle of henna on Menachem's palm, telling him he would always be an honored and blessed member of my family, it was a special moment. I intercepted a gaze that passed between Ruchama and her bridegroom, reflecting the same feeling I had had for her father. When I put a dab of henna on Sarah's palm, she kissed me and whispered, "Now we really are one family."

My eyes were drawn to the pomegranate pendant. It was eighteen years since Ezra had given it to me on our wedding night, eighteen years – symbolizing *chai,* life.

So much had happened... there had been death as well as life, but still, I had much to be grateful for: a good livelihood, my father living with us in Jerusalem, my children grown and sharing this night's joy, my friends celebrating with us.

The pomegranate pendant glowed in the starlight, not obscured by all the other necklaces, which merely served as a backdrop for its beauty. For me, it was a radiant symbol, not only of fruitfulness for my daughter, but of hope for us all.

Part Two

23

IT WAS MY FORTY-SEVENTH birthday. I looked in the mirror and was not too distressed by what I saw. I was still slim; my hair, still black, was threaded with only a little silver. My attire, as always, was modest, but of late I avoided the colorful prints I had favored in my youth. Now I wore a black skirt and high-necked white linen blouse, with my only jewelry – the pomegranate pendant – on its delicate gold chain.

The necklace had adorned the throats of two more brides since Ruchama's wedding twelve years earlier. Assaf had married Tirtza, a Yemenite girl, and they now had four children. To the great delight of both me and Djeddi – who was now becoming very frail at seventy-eight – Shalom had finally settled down too, and had married Rina, Yifat and Reuven's youngest daughter.

After Ruchama's marriage, Shalom had not returned to work in Beit Lechem, although he refused to go back to school. Instead, with some behind-the-scenes manipulation by Djeddi, he was offered a job by a Jewish building contractor called Ya'akov Mann. Everyone called Mann "the building Rabbi," but the Yemenites called him "Father," for he had begun employing Yemenite stonecutters instead of Arabs, thereby providing many of our countrymen with a livelihood. Shalom eventually became his foreman.

I knew Shalom would never be a scholar or a silversmith; he needed heavy, physical work to satisfy that restlessness within him. However, when Nissim Bektar opened his Alliance vocational school, my son finally found an academic niche for himself. The school offered afternoon and evening classes in crafts specifically related to the existing Jerusalem economy, such as carpentry and furniture-making. Bektar gave Shalom a part-time teaching position in the classes in stonecutting, masonry and metalwork, classes which were attended by large numbers of Yemenite and Sephardi Jews, and even some Arabs.

The transformation that had taken place with my youngest child was wonderful to behold. On the afternoons that he gave classes, he would come home early from his work for Rabbi Mann at Abraham's Vineyard, remove his dirty overalls, and wash very carefully, emerging twenty minutes later in dark trousers, a white shirt and polished shoes. As he strode off to teach, his head would be held high and his shoulders straight. I would look at my father and smile, and without a word, he would nod slowly. It was as if we were both saying: "You see, if you only believe, miracles can happen." I hoped that somehow my Ezra would know that I'd heeded his warning to watch out for this son, and that our efforts had been rewarded.

Now that he was married, Shalom lived with Rina in a small stone cottage in Kfar Shiloach, near her parents. Yifat and Reuven had indeed moved into their new house, and since we had made her a partner in *The Pomegranate Pendant,* they no longer had to fear poverty and were even able to help their seven children as they grew up.

My business was supporting a lot of people. My Ashkenazi son-in-law Menachem, who was a scribe like Assaf, wrote *mezuzot* which were sold in my shop in beautiful silver scroll cases that Djeddi still made. Yifat and her daughter-in-law, Evyatar's wife, supplied me with embroidered challah covers as well as headscarves, children's dresses and tablecloths. Ruchama, her eyesight fully restored, still painted and her scenes of Jerusalem were in great demand by tourists. Assaf's wife supplied me with crocheted baby clothes, and I continued making traditional Yemenite jewelry. Djeddi also created exquisite pieces, but at his age he tired easily. I wanted him to retire, but he found the suggestion so hurtful that I never spoke of it again. Often, though, he would take an afternoon off to sit and learn with his friend *Mori* Saadyah, traveling the short distance back and forth to Kfar Shiloach by carriage.

There were now over 170 families in Shiloach. In fact, by 1914, twice as many Jerusalemites lived outside the Old City as within its walls. There were 70,000 people in the city, 45,000 of whom were Jews. My friend Sarah, who at seventy was still ambitious for me, tried to persuade me to relocate my store to Jaffa Road, Jerusalem's main thoroughfare and accessible to a broader clientele, but I had no interest in moving.

Jaffa Road was very modern now, lined not only with Jewish houses, but also foreign consulates and Shaare Zedek Hospital, where Dr. Wallach was now director. There were European post offices, shops, and several hotels catering to the influx of tourists: the Grand New Hotel, kept by a Catholic named Marcos, near the Jaffa Gate; the Central Hotel, just off the main street, run by a Jew named Amdurski; the Park Hotel; and the Hotel Hughes, run by an Englishman. Near the French consulate, there was the Hotel de France, owned by Dominique Bourrel – a sophisticated French-Algerian woman who became one of my best customers and also a good friend. Dominique kept me up-to-date on the Jerusalem social scene, which was useful in my business, and often recommended my shop to her well-heeled guests.

Perhaps, if I had taken Sarah's advice, the shop would have expanded even more, but the Old City location had been lucky for me and my family, and as the Sages tell us: "Change your plot – change your lot." I didn't want my "lot" to change, Heaven forbid, for the worse! I felt sheltered and protected by the walls, and although I sometimes went shopping in Jaffa Road with Ruchama or one of my daughters-in-law, the Rova felt like home to me and I was never tempted to move.

Ruchama and Menachem lived in Meah She'arim with their five children, most of whom were fair like their Ashkenazi father. The youngest, however – little Miriam, aged two – was a miniature of my daughter and I doted on her. Her skin was coffee satin, her eyes black coals, and her dark hair grew in ringlets. Grandmothers are not allowed to have favorites, but she was special – not boisterous like the other children but quiet and sensitive. Young as she was, she responded to beautiful things. I always took life a day at a time, but when I would look at Miriam, I couldn't help but hope I would live to fasten the pomegranate pendant around her neck when the time came for her to marry.

There were more concerns than my immediate family in those disturbing days: despite our rather insular existence, we Jews were not unaware of the clouds of war on the horizon. True, the Turks persecuted us, but "Better a devil you know than one you don't."

Britain had established a consulate in Jerusalem long before I came to live here – in 1838, I was told. Many others followed. The consuls of all the Entente countries left one by one at the start of what came to be known as the Great War; as part of the Turkish Empire, Palestine was inevitably swept up in it. In October 1914, Britain declared war on Turkey.

In the early part of the year, there was regularly a British visitor to my shop, a young man named Robert Parker. He was some kind of under-secretary at the British Embassy. He came in so often that I became quite uncomfortable, believing he sought the pleasure of my company rather than a bauble for his girlfriend. He was ten years my junior and obviously a gentile, and although I didn't want to discourage a customer, his frequent visits were almost embarrassing. He usually bought some trifle – never anything expensive – and lingered a long time at a rack of Ruchama's unframed watercolors without purchasing any.

After a while I began to notice a pattern emerging. He always came in an hour after another customer, whom I addressed as Effendi Husseini. He was a Moslem Arab, the son of the Mufti of Gaza, and he had intimate connections with the Turks, whose garrison in Jerusalem consisted of an entire battalion housed at Schneller Woods. I never seemed to have on display what Husseini was looking to buy, and I would always have to go to the storeroom to search among our surplus stock, leaving the shop unattended for a few minutes. Djeddi, his back to the customers and intent on his work, was oblivious to these goings-on. When I returned, what I brought would never be exactly what Husseini had asked for and he would leave in great haste. At first I suspected that he was stealing, but there was never anything missing.

One night I discussed these two clients with Djeddi and Shalom, who had always possessed a quick mind. "I don't think it's a coincidence, Imma," he said thoughtfully. "Do you think Husseini might be a spy and is leaving a message for Mr. Parker somewhere in your shop? Perhaps he's spying for the British?"

Suddenly everything fell into place. I now realized why it was essential for Husseini to send me to the back of the store. The next time he came in, I watched very carefully where he'd positioned himself: just near the rack of paintings. As I stepped into the back room, I surreptitiously looked back to see him place an envelope between two of the watercolors. I pretended not to have seen, and perhaps he was not aware that I had, but he did purchase something this time, possibly to allay my suspicions.

After he left, I rushed to Djeddi and told him what had transpired. "Should I open the envelope?" I asked him.

"To what purpose, Mazal?"

"Perhaps I should let the Turks know that Husseini is giving information to the British."

"What concern of ours is it?" he sighed. "Turks, British – until the Mashiach reigns and we are again masters in our own Land, who the rulers are makes little difference to the Jews. They all oppress us."

I knew Djeddi was right. The Turks were bad; maybe the British would be better. Or worse. Who knew what lay ahead? Yet I was frightened that *The Pomegranate Pendant* was being used as a drop-off place for messages. If the Turks found out, they might not believe that I was not involved.

An hour later, right on cue, Robert Parker strolled into the shop, his usual charming self.

"You look very nice today, madam," he greeted me, bowing slightly at the waist.

"Thank you," I replied a bit stiffly. I stepped over to a spot right next to the rack of paintings; he browsed in a distant part of the shop.

"I'd like to see those," he said, pointing to the far

corner.

"Those are *tefillin,*" I told him, not moving.

He looked nonplused. "Yes, I'd like to see them."

"Do you know what they are?"

He shuffled his feet nervously. "I will when you explain it."

I shook my head. "They are phylacteries, leather boxes with straps that Jewish men wear at prayer. I don't think they would interest you, really."

I still hadn't moved. He looked wildly to another corner where the children's embroidered dresses were. "Perhaps a dress, for my niece..."

"Please feel free to go and look through them," I suggested, staying where I was.

By this time, he realized something was wrong. He looked at me levelly. "Perhaps you have something of mine?"

"Perhaps."

"Do you want money for it?"

"No."

"What do you want?"

"Mr. Parker," I said with all the force I could muster, "I want that neither you nor Effendi Husseini should enter my shop again. I do not want to be involved, even innocently, in any intrigue. Do you understand?"

His face went red. "Are you such a lover of the Turks, madam, that you are loyal to them?"

"I am loyal only to God and to my people," I answered coolly, although my heart was racing.

"You would be better off under the British, you know that?"

"There have been many conquerors of Jerusalem, Mr. Parker, each worse than the one before. I have no love for the Turks who have been masters here for 400 years. But I know nothing of your people either."

He lowered his voice. "You help me, madam, and when the British take Jerusalem – and we will – it will go well for you and your family."

"No, Mr. Parker," I said firmly, "I will not help you, but neither will I betray you. Please collect your envelope among the paintings, and then tell Effendi Husseini that he will have to find somewhere else to leave his messages."

The genial expression I was accustomed to seeing vanished completely. Steely blue eyes looked back at me. "Filthy Jewess," were the words he spat out as he turned on his heel and slammed the door of my shop. I never saw him again.

24

WHAT DJEDDI HAD SAID
was true: no matter who conquered
Jerusalem, the Jews suffered at their hands.
The Turks had been our rulers for four centuries.
At first, they had treated Palestine well and their sultan,
Suleiman had built the walls and gates still standing in
the Old City. But after he died, the empire began to decay
and Jerusalem sank along with it. Around the time we
had come to live here, a recovery had started – not because
of the Turks, but because of competition among the
European powers with interests here. France supported
Jerusalem's Catholics; the Prussians and the English
together established a Protestant presence; and the Czar
of Russia became patron of the Greek Orthodox.

The Jews had a patron too at that time, but it was
not a country. It was just one man: Sir Moses Monetfiore,
an outstanding English philanthropist. A true advocate
of the Jewish people, he died shortly after we came to the
Old City. We had once considered living in his "quiet
dwelling place" – Mishkenot Sha'ananim, the residential
area which he'd established outside the walls as a haven
for Jewish settlers. He even built a windmill there, to
enable residents to earn a living grinding wheat into flour.
Only our fear of bandits at night had stopped us from
settling there, for we felt the impregnable walls were our
protection.

And now, four centuries of Ottoman rule were
drawing to a close. We were neither happy nor sad, having
no reason to believe the British would be kinder to us

despite Robert Parker's assertion. When he was thwarted, he'd shown himself to be as much of an anti-Semite as the others, despite his earlier honeyed words.

On the verge of defeat, the Turks became desperate. Our population was depleted by 25,000. It is an awesome figure especially in such a close community where we all knew one another. Several thousand Jews, including some of our friends, were deported northward to Constantinople. Disease and death did not discriminate and both Jews and Arabs died of famine. Food was scarce; even my money was not much help.

One day, when I'd been able to purchase some bags of flour and rice at a ridiculously high price, I went to Meah Shea'rim to distribute food to some poor neighbors of Ruchama's. Upon my return, a most dreadful sight greeted me outside the Jaffa Gate. I ran all the way to Sarah's house, sobbing in great, convulsive gulps, and quaking with terror. She opened the door to my frantic pounding.

"Mazal, what is it?" she asked, alarmed.

"I saw... men hanging... outside Jaffa Gate...

She put her arm around me and led me inside.

"The Turks are desperate, driven into a corner," she told me solemnly. "They are making an example of what they call traitors."

"There were five of them!" I exclaimed, my eyes still wide with horror.

"I know," she said softly. "The whole Rova is talking about it. One was a Jewish soldier, Yosef Amozek. He'd been conscripted into the Turkish army. All he did was leave his unit to visit his sick mother in Jerusalem."

"And the others?" I could barely speak.

"They were Arabs caught working for the British. Two were Christians and the other two were Moslems –

the Mufti of Gaza and his son, members of the Husseini family."

I looked at her in shock. So Effendi Husseini, who so furtively left notes to be picked up by Robert Parker, had been caught. The fact that I knew him somehow made it more horrible. I realized what would have happened to me had the Turks discovered that my store was the conduit for his espionage activities. The thought made me ill.

Wherever I went in Jerusalem, tragic sights assaulted my eyes. I had accumulated a lot of money over the years but it was worthless in the fight against malaria and typhus. Disease was rampant in the city. In one dreadful year, over two thousand Jews had died of typhus fever. It was good that I'd put money aside, though, because few customers came to *The Pomegranate Pendant* during those war years. My savings was all we had. Djeddi now lived with me at the Chosh, as we'd rented out the back of the shop to a poor family. He still insisted on working for the few hours each day that the shop was open, but jewelry was the last thing on peoples' minds as they searched for food to survive. I still grew herbs and a few vegetables and often in the mornings I would go to pick them, only to find that some desperate soul had come in the night and stripped the garden of everything edible.

The war raged on for three long years. Many Jewish soldiers were fighting with the British, who were advancing from the Suez Canal, while Arabs fought along the desert railway south of Damascus. But news from the front meant little. We still knew nothing of what our lot would be when the fighting ended.

I was fifty years old – older than my mother had been when she died, and certainly older than the Jewish women I remembered in Sana'a, whom I'd thought were very old when I was a young bride of fifteen. I didn't feel or look old, I thought, but I was weary. I knew that Djeddi would not be with me for many more years. His eyesight was failing and he was very thin. I longed to make him strong nourishing soups – the *marak regel* that he loved – and the spicy Yemenite meats to tempt his waning appetite, but the ingredients were unobtainable. The Turkish army took all the food, and we were lucky to have bread, rice and sometimes a few vegetables.

I fretted about living alone in the future and began to think I was wrong not to have remarried. My friends at first had tried their hand at matchmaking, but when they realized that I considered Ezra my first and only husband, they gave up attempting to find me a *shidduch*. Yet the idea of living with one of my married children, as much as I loved them, was horrific to me. In Yemen it would have been natural for an extended family to live together: the grandmother would help care for the little ones and the household, sharing the mother's burden. Even in Jerusalem among Ashkenazi families this was not uncommon. But my children were all managing quite well on their own, praise God. My presence would be an intrusion.

When Ezra died, I had been compelled by circumstances to break with tradition. I had become the breadwinner, a silversmith, a businesswoman, and a woman of property. I could speak many languages, and I could read and write. I knew that my father still disapproved. He foresaw that I would be lonely when he passed on. My life had not been easy, but it had been fulfilling and the inactivity forced on me by the war was galling.

In that November of 1917, despite the cold and hunger, we experienced a surge of hope when the Balfour

Declaration was issued. A translation of it appeared in our newspapers, stating that the British Government favored "the establishment in Palestine of a National Home for the Jewish People."

"If the British win this war, do you think they will really let us be our own masters?" I asked Djeddi. Robert Parker's insult still echoed painfully in my ears, yet my optimism had not completely died.

Djeddi shrugged his thin shoulders. "If it comes about, it will be the will of the Almighty, not of man. Many of our prophets wrote of it. Yechezkel prophesied: 'Thus says the Lord God: I will even gather you from the nations, and assemble you out of the countries where you have been scattered, and I will give you the Land of Israel.' We do not need the blessing of the British," he concluded scornfully. "It was promised to us by the Almighty Himself."

The fighting continued relentlessly. On the 7th of November, the British drove the Turks from Gaza, and nine days later they pushed them out of Jaffa. The British began their advance towards Jerusalem, but on November 25th, they were halted by a strong Turkish counterattack. Like the war, our hope ebbed and flowed as the tide shifted.

Cold, poverty, hunger, disease and death – they were the lot of the Jews in those dark wintry days. When would "Judah and Israel dwell in safety, each man under his vine and under his fig tree..."?

25

JERUSALEM WAS A
BLEAK, abandoned city. One
by one, all the ambassadors and
consuls and their staff had returned to
their countries, except for the American and
Spanish consuls, who stayed on as neutral
representatives to observe the action of the Turks.
Epidemics, famine, arrests and expulsions were the
routine of our daily lives. Sarah lost her husband to
typhoid just as I had, and I spent all the time I could spare
away from Djeddi comforting her and my son-in-law
Menachem. The grief in our household was profound.

Yes, all through the centuries, foreign powers had
coveted Jerusalem and had gone to war to conquer it. In
a way it was ironic – Jerusalem is a poor city with no
resources. Its very name seems a misnomer...the first time
it is mentioned in the Torah, it is called *Shalem,* the city
of Peace. Then Avraham *Avinu,* standing on Har Moriyah,
the future site of the *Beit Ha-mikdash,* called it *Yireh* –
"God will see." Thus it became *Yerushalayim* – Jerusalem.

And yet, despite the many nations coveting it, no
foreign ruler had ever made the city his capital. Some
European kings called themselves by the title "King of
Jerusalem," but it was a meaningless phrase. Even when
it had been known as "the Crusader Kingdom of
Jerusalem," it was not a capital, but simply a military
outpost. Only to the Jewish People was it ever the core
of our existence and the seat of sovereign rule.

Endless conquerors through history...and now it

seemed that Turkish dominion would give way to British. We watched solemnly that Shabbat morning of December 9th, 1917 as the mayor of Jerusalem – another member of the influential Husseini family – wearing a tarbush and leaning heavily on a walking stick, with the Chief of Police at his side, left the city bearing a white flag of surrender. We later learned that they walked to a hill overlooking Mei Neftoach, which the Arabs called Lifta, but the only British they could find to surrender to were two astounded low-ranking officers, Sergeants Hurcomb and Sedgewick of the 2/19th Battalion, London Regiment, who happened to be there because they were looking for water. Even in surrender, the Turks looked ridiculous.

The next day, however, Major General Shea, General Officer commanding the British 66th Division, officially received the Turks' surrender in the gardens of Shaare Zedek Hospital on Jaffa Road. A day after that, General Allenby made his official entrance into the city with much pomp. He was accompanied by representatives of the French and Italian contingents which had fought on the Jerusalem front. It was a dignified ceremony, somewhat restrained as the British had lost 3,600 soldiers. The Turkish losses had been staggering – 19,000 soldiers, they said, had been killed in action.

Jerusalem had fallen to the British, but it was not the end of the war. There were nine frightening months to follow, when the front line lay only 12 miles north of our city. During this time, wherever you walked, there were British armored cars to be seen.

The future was so uncertain. In every *beit knesset* fervent prayers were offered, invoking the Almighty's benevolence. We felt rather like children who had been put up for adoption. We had no fond memories of the Ottoman regime, yet it was familiar and at least we knew the limits of their corruption and cruelty. Our new masters were courteous and correct, but their intentions toward us were shrouded in mystery. As always, our fate was in God's hands, but even those whose *bitachon* was strong experienced anxiety.

If not for the demands of business, I would have been ill with worry, but the British soldiers wanted to buy souvenirs for their wives, girlfriends and families back home, so once again *The Pomegranate Pendant* was open full-time. At the very least, with so many people dependent on me for their livelihood, I was fulfilling my responsibilities; it also served to distract me from the larger concerns.

In September, the British troops advanced first to Shechem and then moved on to take Damascus and Aleppo, before the Turks surrendered totally on December 31, 1918. For the gentile British troops stationed in Jerusalem, it was a New Year's Eve and victory celebration combined, with loud music and gaiety.

Among the British troops were many Jewish soldiers, and we were delighted to see them sometimes worshipping in our *beit knesset* or praying at the *Kotel*. Their presence allayed many of our fears. We began to feel it would be a kindlier regime than that of the Turks, and at first it certainly seemed so: the British military authorities repaired and widened the rail line to the coast. They also built a narrow-gauge railway to carry their supplies. In the Old City, they began to repair the walls and gates that had been damaged. The British Military Governor, Ronald Storrs, seemed to show unaccustomed sensitivity by forbidding the demolition of ancient or historic buildings, so our holy places were preserved. He also insisted that any new construction be of Jerusalem stone, to preserve the city's heritage and tradition.

It seemed the British were determined to leave their mark everywhere they went. All around the Old City and its environs, they established their presence. And it was all happening so fast. From customers and acquaintances I received regular reports of their progress: to the north was a Military Governate at Schmidt College, and there were army camps in the Kidron Valley and near the Augusta Victoria Hospital. They set up soldiers' hostels, military stores and clearing hospitals to the west, taking over the Fast Hotel for their Army and Navy Canteen Board. There was an ice factory serving them just near the Ashpot Gate where my store was located, while to the south they had set up communications centers, ordnance stores and airstrips to land Royal Air Force planes.

Although there were many British and Indian soldiers standing guard throughout the Old City, the first acts of the British Mandate seemed to aim for peaceful co-existence. They brought piped water into Jerusalem from the south. This was wonderful! The Turks had never tried to improve our lot, which was why disease had been so rife. We had taken our water from rainwater cisterns when we could, or else it was brought into the Old City from the well at *Ein Rogel*, in filthy goatskins. I had always boiled it – perhaps intuitively because we knew little of hygiene – which is how I'd managed to keep my family healthier than most.

We truly appreciated the piped water, which Sarah said was the first adequate supply the city had known since the Romans had brought water from the south by aqueduct. The British water pipeline ran from *Bereichot Shelomo*, with the main distribution lines from a reservoir in Romema that supplied the entire population. We not only had unlimited clean drinking water, we could do laundry whenever we pleased and even water our small gardens.

Ruchama's five children all loved to spend Shabbat with us in the Old City, either with Bubbie Sarah or Savta Mazal and Djeddi. Her eldest daughter, Leah, was now fourteen and a very serious girl who took good care of her three brothers, Netanel, Yoel and Yosef, and her baby sister Miriam. Ruchama and Menachem enjoyed the opportunity to spend an occasional Shabbat on their own in Meah She'arim, so some of the children slept in my home and some at Sarah's and we'd have Shabbat dinner together. The British had introduced food rationing which at least allowed some food to reach us instead of it all going to the Turkish army as it had before the Mandate. We had starved during the war when wheat supplies were cut off, but under Governor Storrs things improved – not a great quantity or wide variety of food, but enough basics to let us make a semblance of Shabbat meals again.

When the children came it was a story-time. Djeddi would try to instill in them a love of Yemenite tradition while Sarah, not to be outdone, would regale them with stories from the villages of Europe, the shtetls. After the Shabbat meal, Djeddi gathered them around the table, with little Miriam sitting on his knee. She was the only one that looked truly Yemenite, and Djeddi – who could be very stern at times with the children – treated her with touching gentleness.

"Where did we go to pray this morning?" he asked them.

Eleven-year-old Netanel was the first to answer. "Beit El." It was the *beit knesset* in Jerusalem that Djeddi favored.

"What does it mean?"

"The House of God," answered Leah.

He nodded. "Here all the *mekubalim* of Jerusalem come together to study the mystical secrets of the Torah." When he had captured their attention, and they'd stopped fidgeting, he continued: "This Beit El was the *beit knesset* of the great Yemenite rabbi, *Morenu* Sar Shalom Sharabi, 200 years ago. Do you know who used to sit next to him?"

"Abba?" ventured little Miriam.

Djeddi laughed. "No, it was Eliyahu *Ha-Navi* No one else could see Eliyahu, but he would tell Rav Sar Shalom all the secrets of the Torah and its hidden mysteries. Rav Sar Shalom had a servant woman, and one day she brought him two cups of coffee. He looked at her questioningly. 'The other cup is for the man beside you,' she said. 'This is Eliyahu *Ha-Navi,*' he whispered, 'but it is a secret – you must tell no one.' She agreed, on condition that she be promised a place in *Gan Eden* next to Rav Sar Shalom."

"Did he promise?" Leah asked, her eyes wide with wonder.

"Yes, he did," Djeddi replied.

"Did Eliyahu drink his coffee?" Miriam wanted to know.

Before we got up from the table, Sarah took up the storytelling. "I want to tell you about Meah She'arim, where you live. Do you know what it means?"

"It means a hundred gates," Yoel said confidently, "but I tried counting them and there aren't even fifty!"

Sarah laughed. "The word *'she'arim'* has another meaning. I'll give you a hint: you'll find it in *parashat Toldot.*"

Netanel, smart as a whip, immediately quoted the correct verse: "And Yitzchak sowed in that land and found in the same year a hundredfold – *meah she'arim* – and Hashem blessed him."

"That's right," Bubbie Sarah said. "From each grain of wheat that Yitzchak planted, he reaped a hundred more. That number was the symbol of plenty. The first settlers in your neighborhood wanted to see their number increase rapidly, so they chose the name, Meah She'arim."

I sat there watching my family, my heart overflowing... Djeddi, frail as he was, sitting at the head of the table in his long, colorful robes, dressed as he had always dressed in Yemen; Sarah was wearing her usual high-collared, no-nonsense cotton dress, sturdy black boots and a turban – today it was a white one with gold beads, in honor of Shabbat. And there were my grandchildren: four of them tall and fair like Menachem with his European ancestry, and dainty Miriam, a dark miniature of Ruchama. It did indeed signify the Ingathering of the Exiles.

I toyed with the gold pomegranate pendant and thought of the fruit with its many seeds. My fruitfulness had borne this strange multi-cultural family, with different traditions but one heritage, sharing the same future in our holy Land – Eretz Yisrael.

26

YOM KIPPUR 5691. I had accompanied Sarah to the Tiferet Synagogue, as at her age, it was difficult for her to walk there alone. Although I was some twenty years younger, I also found myself tiring easily these days. I would really have preferred to pray at Beit El where my father had felt so at home, but Tiferet Yisrael was Sarah's family synagogue, so in a way it was mine as well. Besides, she had insisted on fasting and I was worried that she might collapse. During the recent riots in Chevron she had suffered some terrible family losses and all her strength and will to live seemed to be leaving her.

From the window of the *beit knesset,* I could see right to the site of the ancient Holy Temple, lost to us for nearly two thousand years. "So many losses," I thought to myself, as the *Yizkor* service, the Memorial for the Dead, began.

> *O Lord, what is man, that You regard him? Or the son of man, that You reckon with him? Man is like a breath; his days are as a shadow that passes away. In the morning he blooms and sprouts afresh; by the evening he is cut down and withers...*

Silently my tears began to flow for Djeddi, my beloved father, who had left me nine years before. He had lived to eighty-five, but still his days seemed like a shadow to me. I had come to depend on him as the head of my family, the elder. He had continued to make beautiful jewelry for my store up to the day of his death. But more than that, he had been the keeper of the Yemenite tradition for my family, the one who had taught my children and grandchildren to nurture it as a special possession, the one who had kept the flame burning. He was the teller of tales, the weaver of enchantment. He never adapted to Western dress nor made any other concession to the fact that we had left Yemen behind. Until the day he died, he prayed wrapped in the prayer shawl he had brought from Sana'a over the flowing robes he had brought from Sana'a, his white beard and long sidecurls swaying with the motion of his body. He had studied Torah with his friends and had taught us all to thank God for the bad as for the good, for everything the Almighty does is good. He'd never compromised his principles, yet he had been a gentle and compassionate man who encouraged me to be charitable, especially to our Yemenite brethren.

So teach us to number our days, that
we may acquire a heart of wisdom...

Ezra, my beloved husband, had known so few days. At only twenty-six years of age he had returned his soul to his Maker. I had been a widow for forty-one years, yet I could still close my eyes and recall my Ezra in every last detail. He had already had a heart of wisdom even then, or perhaps God had given him the gift of prophecy, for he'd warned me what lay ahead: Ruchama's frailty and sensitivity; Assaf's swift mind that needed nurturing; Shalom's strong-willed waywardness. Without his foresight, perhaps the job of raising the children alone would have been even more difficult for me.

> *Mark the innocent man, and behold*
> *the upright; for the end of that man is*
> *peace...*

My mind turned to my dear mother, whom I'd last seen when I was only fifteen, a young bride about to leave Sana'a for the frightening journey to the Holy Land. I prayed that she had found peace. She had worked so hard caring for her ten children, and tending the herbs and folk wisdom to keep our family, friends and neighbors healthy. I had believed we would be reunited in Jerusalem, but the Turks had kept delaying permission for my father to leave Yemen until it was too late. By then my mother had already left us.

> *...And the dust returns to the earth*
> *as it was, but the spirit returns to God Who*
> *gave it....*

I wondered how much longer I still had to live. I didn't want to bear any more losses, especially that of my dear friend Sarah, now standing beside me, her once sturdy body so frail and shrunken. But her mind was as strong as ever. Suddenly I remembered a Yiddish proverb she had taught me: *"Az men dermont-zikh on dem toit, iz men nit zikher mitn lebn* – Begin thinking of death and you are no longer sure of your life." I smiled, reached out and squeezed her hand.

I still had much to live for. I had fifteen grandchildren, *b'li ayin ha-ra:* Ruchama's five, Assaf's four and Shalom's six – he had finally surpassed his siblings at something! He continued to teach at the Alliance School and was a good husband and father. He had one son though, ten-year-old Mattanyah, who reminded me so much of Shalom at that age, that I was tempted to tell him that it was time even now to curb the boy's high spirits. But I knew he would just laugh at me, so I kept my counsel, although I would have loved to discipline him a little bit myself.

The grandchild closest to me was still Miriam, Ruchama's youngest daughter, now aged eighteen. Perhaps because of her Yemenite looks, or perhaps because she had been given my mother's name, she was especially dear to me. She also visited me the most often. I knew that as soon as the shofar was blown to signify the end of Yom Kippur, she would be on her way to the Old City to visit her two grandmothers and make sure we were all right.

Miriam was studying to be a nurse at Shaare Zedek, the hospital still headed by the wonderful Dr. Wallach who had saved her mother's sight. She was very delicate and slender, and it was heavy work, but she had grown up learning about her great-grandmother's herbal remedies and she too wanted to help heal people. Ruchama had encouraged her to apply at Shaare Zedek where the Head Nurse, Schwester Selma, who had come from Germany to assist Dr. Wallach, was reputed to be the best, and strictest, nurse in all of Palestine.

The past year, 1929, had been one of the most dreadful I remembered. Miriam told me of the many typhoid, typhus and meningitis cases that had been hospitalized at Shaare Zedek. To protect herself from infection, she'd been given white laborer's overalls with a hood to cover her hair. But much worse by far had been the terrible massacre of Jews in Chevron by their Arab neighbors – some of whom had seemed to be their friends for years and whose children had played together! The Arabs, wielding long knives, had raided the yeshivah in Chevron. There were a number of young American boys among the students. Miriam had been part of the team sent there by Shaare Zedek to help evacuate the wounded, a terrifying experience for a young girl. Many of the bodies were mutilated, some even dismembered! May the Almighty avenge their blood.

This had been the culmination of a long series of Arab attacks since the British Mandate had taken effect. The British troops were supposed to be defending us, but we didn't feel protected. The attack in Chevron and on individual Jews in Palestine had been inflamed by a leaflet full of scurrilous lies, distributed all over the country, signed by "The Jerusalem Arab Students" and dated September 11th, 1929. There had even been one tacked to the door of my shop. It read:

> 0 Arab! Remember that the Jew is your strongest enemy and the enemy of your ancestors since olden times. Do not be misled by his tricks for it is he who... poisoned Mohammed, peace and worship be with him. It is he who now endeavors to slaughter you as he did yesterday. Be aware that the best way to save yourself and your Fatherland from the grasp of the foreign intruder and greedy Jew is to boycott him... and support the industry of your Fatherland.

It had begun a year ago, in quite a small way. The Arabs protested that we should not have the right to the

Holy Places, and insisted that the *Kotel* was also holy to them, although why they should be interested in the last remnant of our Holy Temple was beyond understanding. The Mufti of Jerusalem, Hajj Amin al-Husseini – the worst foe of the Jews – used this excuse to muster his followers, young fanatics whose religious hatred of us was easily fanned until it went out of control. He persuaded them that the Jews also had designs on their holy places and urged them to mount a *jihad* – a holy war.

In August, just two months ago, Arab mobs tried to attack us here in the Rova. They were repulsed by the Haganah, but the violence spread all over the country. They rampaged in Kfar Shiloach and the village had to be evacuated. In Motza they slaughtered an entire family – parents and children, uncles and cousins. The victims of bloodthirsty Arabs were everywhere.

Sarah's daughter Naomi, who was my age, lived in Chevron with her family. Her husband taught in the yeshivah and her married son Ya'akov learned there. After she fled to Jerusalem, she sobbed out her story to her mother, whom I was visiting at the time. Like Sarah, she'd always been a strong woman, not given to bouts of hysteria. I couldn't believe that this wretched, wild-eyed woman was the same person I'd stood in awe of for so many years. As we listened to her story, we soon understood the transformation. We cried and clung to each other, overcome with grief and fear.

"It happened on Shabbat," she told us, reliving the nightmare. "We had just come home from services, when there were these blood-curdling cries. I looked out the window and saw a mob being led by Ibrahim – our neighbor. I couldn't believe it! When my children were little, they had played with him. We had invited him to our home on Pesach because he loved to eat matza. My son Ya'akov was his friend, and now Ya'akov's children played with his children." Her voice faltered, tears coursing down her cheeks. "The mob broke down our door. Ibrahim had a knife. He killed Ya'akov, and my husband, and Ya'akov's little girl, my beautiful granddaughter Batya. And he laughed – he enjoyed it! He looked in my eyes and he laughed!"

Chevron was a small, defenseless Jewish community. The mob slaughtered seventy men, women and children on that terrible Shabbat. Even infants were butchered. Naomi and what was left of her family and the few other survivors, some two hundred, all told, were evacuated to Jerusalem.

Chevron was not the only place to fall victim to the Arab murderers. Their attacks on Tel Aviv and the Jewish quarter of Haifa were repulsed, but five days later the mobs struck again in Tzefat, killing eighteen Jews and wounding dozens more before the Jews could take refuge in the police headquarters while the murderers ransacked and burned down the Jewish quarter. Only by hiding in a cowshed were the settlers of Be'er Toviya saved; the mob plundered and destroyed the village before attacking Chulda, where a handful of Jewish defenders held out for hours against thousands of Arabs. They only escaped when a British patrol finally arrived to rescue them, and then the Arabs destroyed their settlement.

When the Balfour Declaration was announced back in 1917, the Jews had been euphoric. Yitzchak Breuer, a leader of Agudat Yisrael, had rejoiced, as did many other prominent religious personalities. But it had not been an altruistic document intended for our benefit; we were simply pawns. The British thought that by sponsoring a national home for the Jews, they could forestall French control of Palestine. I had talked about it all those years ago with Sarah.

"It will be good for us, Sarah," I had maintained. "The British will protect us until we can rule ourselves." How naive I had been.

Sarah had dismissed my remark with derision. "It is a fig leaf, this Declaration. They don't want us to have self-rule. They just pretend so that they can occupy Palestine instead of the Turks and won't have to give any of it to France."

"Why would they want Palestine, with their vast empire?"

Sarah shrugged. "Empires fall sometimes. Anyway, it's handy for the defense of the Suez Canal and for imperial communications on the route to India. They want us to look after their interests in the Middle East."

For the first time, I doubted Sarah's sagacity. Everyone had rejoiced at the Balfour Declaration... Why was she so negative?

She shook her finger at me. "Don't forget the British also promised the Hashemites a post-war Arab liberation – and they think that means Palestine."

"But Lord Balfour gave us the plan because of Chaim Weizmann," I said, genuinely puzzled.

"He believed what Weizmann said, that Zionism had the support of all the Jews in Russia and America. Because of this, he felt it was a way to keep us loyal to the Allies during the war. You see, the British Foreign Office was worried that the Jews were pro-Germany. Like many gentiles, they believe that Jews all over the world wield tremendous power and influence. Have you heard of Sir Mark Sykes?" I shook my head.

"Well, he helped Balfour to formulate the Declaration. He told him that Jews could be manipulated to serve British needs – in America, Russia, everywhere."

As always, I was impressed by Sarah's knowledge and ability to assess situations. In the end, it had been the Bolsheviks who came to power in Russia and the Jews among them denounced all imperialist land grabs, including the British conquest of Palestine. Jews like Trotsky rose to power there and they hated the notion of Zionism.

Sarah had always credited me with more insight than I really possessed. She tried to make me understand. "The British thought of the Jews as pro-German financiers," she explained patiently. I nodded. Many German Jews had indeed fought for the Kaiser and I remembered, a little guiltily, how grateful I had been to Prince Adalbert for his help in getting permission for my father to leave Yemen.

"Perhaps I am too cynical, Mazal," she said after a pause. "Maybe some British statesmen *were* idealistic. After all, as Christians, they see the Bible as a living reality, and perhaps restoring the Jewish homeland is something they feel is morally correct. Yes, maybe I'm too cynical."

But her cynicism had been in place. Events had unfortunately proved her right. Even the British Jews had not been happy about the Balfour Declaration. Well entrenched in English society, they didn't want to be suspected of having dual loyalties. And now, a dozen years later, Sarah had to live with the bitterness that the massacres had wrought: her daughter widowed, her son-in-law, grandson, and great-granddaughter brutally slaughtered, a family that would never forget the horror – while the British authorities had done too little, too late. The Arabs had achieved their end. They had focused the light of political debate on Palestine once again.

Unbelievably, a Parliamentary commission of inquiry headed by Sir Walter Shaw, which was sent to look into the cause of the outbreak, tried to justify the attacks by claiming that they had been provoked by "Arab feelings of animosity and hostility to Jews consequent upon the disappointment of their political and national aspirations and fear for their economic future." The British decided to reward the murderers by restricting Jewish immigration and the purchase of land from the Arabs.

No, the Balfour Declaration had not signaled an era of peace. We were still waiting for real peace to come, and when the British disappointed us, we found our consolation in the Prophet Yeshayahu's promise:

> Rejoice with Jerusalem,
> and be glad with her
> all those who love her;
> rejoice for joy with her,
> all that mourn for her...
> For thus says the Lord:
> Behold, I will extend
> peace to her like a river,
> and the glory of the nations
> like a flowing stream.

We continued to walk the quiet, dark streets of the Rova after the closing *Ne'ilah* prayer of Yom Kippur, Sarah's thin arm linked in mine. The distance was not great, but our pace was slow and my mind went on tracing the events of the past years.

Lord Balfour had been invited to the opening of the Hebrew University of Jerusalem five years before, in 1925. It was a magnificent institution and I couldn't help but hope that some of our yeshivot would one day be built on such a grand scale. I wondered if Harav Avraham Yitzchak Kook, the Ashkenazi Chief Rabbi of Palestine who sat on the dais with all the other dignitaries, had the same thought. The Arabs had demonstrated against the opening and had boycotted the ceremony, which surprised no one. They remained resentful of the British for giving away their "rights" in Palestine to the Jews, and resentful of the Jews for supplanting them.

While we went on with our quiet lives in the Old City, all around the country the Yishuv was expanding and thriving. A hundred new settlements had been established since 1917, including several settled by Chasidim of Kosnitz, Yablona and Lubavitch. For the most part, though, the pioneers were secular Zionists. In each instance, the land was purchased – with the help of philanthropists abroad from the owners, or reclaimed from abandoned Arab villages.

At the same time, we were experiencing a wave of immigration from Europe, and small towns were becoming bustling cities. All sorts of modern things were reaching our distant corner of the world. I remember the day a Zeppelin flew over Jerusalem and parachuted mailbags with letters from Germany. One bag was never found – probably stolen – so, as a result, a handbill was distributed which read: "Keep your eye on the Zeppelin! Today it will fly over Palestine and drop mailbags. Whoever brings an undamaged bag will get a reward of twenty-five shillings." Although I didn't need the reward, I certainly watched the Zeppelin, like a giant bird lumbering across the sky. It both excited and frightened me.

I had the feeling that all these modern inventions were shaking up the world in a physical sense, for just three years ago, there was a powerful earthquake in

Jerusalem. The Church of the Holy Sepulchre, the el-Aksa Mosque and the Augusta Victoria Hospital were all badly damaged, yet miraculously no Jewish home or synagogue was affected.

When Sarah and I reached home, weary and famished from the day's fasting, I was amazed to see the milkman and his donkey making deliveries at night. It was a clever idea of his, for we all wanted fresh milk and he quickly sold all that he had. His donkey bore a sign in three languages – Arabic, English and Hebrew: *Tipat Chalav,* a drop of milk.

Just as I had predicted, Miriam arrived soon after nightfall to see her two grandmothers. After assuring herself that Bubbie Sarah had suffered no ill effects from the fast, she came upstairs to my apartment. She looked beautiful, just as her mother had at that age. I thought of Djeddi and how concerned he would have been that his eighteen-year-old great-granddaughter was still unmarried. He would have been even more concerned to know that it no longer worried me.

"How is my favorite nurse?" I asked her tenderly.

She hugged me. "Back to work tomorrow."

"Is it very hard? Are you sorry you took on such a profession?"

She shook her head. "I have two outstanding examples before me all the time. Neither Dr. Wallach nor Schwester Selma ever look at the clock. Dr. Wallach says: 'The Guardian of Israel neither sleeps nor does He slumber, and neither may we, His humble emissaries.' Whatever needs to be done, must be done; whoever is ill must be treated. No matter how hard I work, it is as nothing compared to them. They both work a fourteen-hour day and then divide the night shift between them."

Chapter Twenty-Six

"But you are just a trainee, a very young girl. You need your sleep."

Miriam smiled at me. "You had two children at my age, and you had made a difficult journey to a new land, leaving your family and everything familiar behind. And you worry about me!"

It was true. I had gone through a great deal by the time I was Miriam's age, but it is human to want things to be easier for one's children, and even more so for one's grandchildren. I knew Schwester Selma's reputation as a perfectionist who was very strict with her nurses, and I wanted Miriam to enjoy her childhood a little longer before she took on the duties of wife and mother. But when I looked at her face, I saw that childhood was already gone. It was the face of a woman.

She took my hand. "Savta, I want to recite a poem for you."

I shook my head. "Your mother is the one for poetry, my dear."

"I know you will like this poem, because it was written by a philosopher and I think it's your philosophy too. Schwester Selma has a framed copy of it over her bed. It reads:

> *I slept and dreamt*
> *That life was joy.*
> *I awoke and saw*
> *That life was duty.*
> *I acted and behold*
> *Duty was joy.*

"That's how I feel, Savta. I'm not a qualified nurse yet, but I'm still helping babies to be born and sick people to get better and old people to be less afraid. It's duty, but it's joy too. And because I am religious I can help all the patients to have *bitachon,* and that alone can hasten their healing."

"I'm proud of you, my darling," I told her, my eyes filled with tears. "Whoever becomes your husband will be very lucky."

"It's not a 'whoever,' Savta. I already know his name."

I waited, unable to speak and disappointed that Ruchama and Menachem had not discussed the matter with me.

"His name is Ya'akov Gershon, and he is a descendant of the famed Rav Avraham Gershon of Kutow – a renowned Chasidic family, related to the Baal Shem Tov himself. We will be married after Chanukah, but he has agreed that I can continue with my nursing until..." she blushed.

"It is indeed a worthy family," I told her. "When Rav Avraham first arrived in Jerusalem, he studied Torah with an illustrious *chevruta – Morenu* Sar Shalom Sharabi."

I could remember my first *tiyul* with Sarah as though it were yesterday. It was the day she restored my pride in my heritage, the day she told me about Rav Avraham and *Morenu* Sar Shalom and the history of the Yishuv.

I tried to be happy for my granddaughter. It was, as she'd said, a renowned family. But an Ashkenazi one. Like her mother, she would leave her traditions a little further behind. Of course, living in Meah She'arim, an Ashkenazi stronghold, it was inevitable, but still I had hoped that just she – of Ruchama's five children – would marry a Yemenite. With her coloring and those big dark eyes, she would have looked so beautiful under a *gargush* at her Chinah ceremony.

She read my thoughts. "Savta, even though it will be an Ashkenazi wedding, I still want to have a Chinah ceremony like all the brides in our family. I want you to dress me, and I want to wear your pomegranate pendant."

I opened my arms to her. There was no need for words.

27

"IF YOU DIDN'T HAVE
SOMETHING to worry about, you'd
invent something," Shalom once told me. It
was true: as a family grows, it is impossible to
worry about each individual member of it and to take
responsibility for all of them. Shalom had given me much
heartache as a boy, but in the end it had come out all
right. Of course I would have preferred for him to learn
in a yeshivah, to study for a suitable profession, or to
become a silversmith and carry on the family tradition.
He had chosen a different path, but he contributed to
society as a builder and a teacher, and he remained
religiously observant, though a bit modern for my taste.
Still my earlier fears had not materialized.

Five of his six children were sturdy, clever and well-
adjusted. At least in marrying Rina, the youngest daughter
of Yifat and Reuven, he had pleased me very much – a
true Yemenite girl raised in our culture. They were very
happy together, and she helped her mother provide stock
for *The Pomegranate Pendant,* those beautifully
embroidered Shabbat tablecloths and challah covers that
were a perpetual favorite of the tourists.

Shalom and Rina were living in a rented apartment
with her parents in a part of the Old City that was called
the Moslem Quarter but in fact was Moslem and Jewish.
Many homes there were owned by Jews. The apartment
was spacious, but had numerous drawbacks, and so the
family was planning to move to one of the new suburbs
in Jerusalem. Governor Storrs and his Pro-Jerusalem

Society had decided some years ago to extend the city boundary and they were building what they termed "Garden Cities" south in Talpiot and west in Bonei Bayit. The latter, which a few years ago had been just empty land full of rocks, was now taking shape with homes and gardens, and it had been given a new name: Belt Hakerem, "the house of the vineyard." Shalom had always hated being closed inside the Old City walls, so the new suburb was very attractive to him. He had started building a home there, but it would take a year to complete as he was doing it himself with just a few laborers to help him.

He called in to see me one afternoon after giving a class at the Alliance School. "How is your house progressing?" I asked him as I poured a cup of the *gisher* he still loved.

He stared moodily at the *manjal,* the open copper brazier that I used to heat my home. Abruptly he rose from the table and began shoveling charcoal into it that it certainly didn't need as it was already glowing red and giving off marvelous warmth. I waited for him to speak. It had taken many years, but now, at sixty-nine, I knew better than to ask too many questions of Shalom. If he wanted to tell me something, he would. If not, my questions would be met with sullen silence. I was an old lady and I had learned the value of patience.

"It is taking too long to build," he answered finally.

"Well, you can't rush these things. What's the hurry?"

"Mattanyah is not happy living with us and Rina's parents. He's never home."

My heart turned over. Matti, the restless one, just like his father. I didn't want to remind him of the heartache he had given me all those years ago, when he was even younger than his sixteen-year-old son.

"Why do you think he's not happy?"

"He hates living among the Arabs. They torment the Jews all the time. Beit Hakerem will be a Jewish suburb. But a year is a long time for a boy to wait. I can't make him understand."

"How is he getting on at school?"

Shalom poked the charcoal savagely. "He's left school – just walked out," he said morosely. I smothered a smile... Hadn't Shalom done the exact same thing?

"What does he want to do? Perhaps he could attend the Alliance School and learn a trade? After all, you teach there."

Shalom shrugged. "I suggested it. He refused. Says he wants some time to think about things without doing anything. The other kids are so easy – they listen to me and Rina, they're no trouble at all. But Matti is one big headache. Imma, do you think he might be a criminal?" he asked suddenly.

"Good heavens!" I was shocked. "What a terrible thing to say about your own son!"

"Imma, he disappears. All hours – sometimes in the middle of the night. He gets a signal... Once I heard someone whistling, and he answered the same way. Another time I saw someone far off with a lantern, making it shine and then covering it, on and off for five minutes. It was three o'clock in the morning! Then I heard Matti go out. I ran after him, asking where he was going, and he just pushed me away and said he needed fresh air. He didn't come home for two days!"

It was no time to remind Shalom of his own past. I could see his eyes were full of tears. Why is it a parent always loves the black sheep just a little more than the obedient children? "Children are difficult at that age," I said slowly, although at sixteen I had been a mother and certainly hadn't thought of myself as a child. "I have an idea, Shalom. If Mattanyah doesn't like living at home, perhaps he'd like to live with me until your new house is ready?"

Shalom's face lit up, but then he shook his head. "It would be too hard for you, Imma. You couldn't handle him. You don't know what he's like."

"But I think he loves me, doesn't he?"

"Yes, he does. But it doesn't mean he'd obey you."

"That's not what I mean. Suppose you told him that at my age, I'm afraid to live on my own and very lonely since my dear Sarah died. Do you think he would come – to protect me?"

Shalom leaned over and kissed my cheek. "You are the best and wisest mother in the world."

I couldn't resist replying: "I wish you'd thought so when you were Mattanyah's age!"

It was easier than we'd expected. Matti couldn't wait to move in with me and his parents were overwhelmingly grateful, although Rina wept when her youngest son left carrying all his possessions in a small, battered suitcase. I told his parents, and his brothers and sisters – Chayim, Tziyona, Bruriya, Nissim and Shulamit – to come and visit him whenever they wished.

"A room to myself!" he cried out happily when I showed him the bedroom which had once been for his father and his uncle Assaf. "I've never had a whole room just for me."

"It's really yours, and completely private," I assured him. "If you undertake to clean it yourself and keep it tidy, I won't even come inside it. I'll give you the only key."

He looked to see if I were serious. I know how important privacy is to a young man," I added seriously.

"Savta Mazal, how come you're the only one in my family who understands me, who treats me like a man?" he asked me later over supper.

"Parents always think of their offspring as children, no matter how old they are. And brothers and sisters – well, you're the youngest, so I guess they will always think of you as the baby of the family. But I can see you're a man. Look how strong you are!" Although I was flattering him to win his confidence, I spoke the truth. He had his father's physique: heavy build, broad shoulders and biceps that strained against the cloth of his sleeves.

He smiled. Then suddenly his mood changed. "Savta, do you trust me?"

"Of course I do," I answered, although I had been seriously perturbed at Shalom's stories about his middle-of-the-night disappearances.

"If you trust me, then I don't want you asking me lots of questions about where I go, who I'm with, what I'm doing. I'm a very private person. I have reasons why I don't want to go to school or work just now. Maybe one day I'll tell you, but not now. Sometimes I go out late at night. Sometimes I stay with friends for a few days..."

"But who will look after me if you're not here?" I asked, trying to make my voice sound plaintive.

Matti smiled impishly. "Savta, you're the strongest, most independent woman in the world. I guessed that it was your idea for me to come here because Abba and Imma couldn't handle me. I went along with it because I wanted to live with you and because you understand me. I'm not a conformist like Chayim and Nissim, but even though I'm younger than my brothers, I'm stronger than both of them and I know more about the world than they do. In my eyes, *they're* the babies, not me."

I sighed. It was almost the same conversation I'd

had with his father about his older brother Assaf all those years ago. "I trust you, Mattanyah, but I have to know some things. When you disappear at night, has it anything to do with girls?"

He laughed. "No, Savta, nothing at all. I promise you."

"Are you doing anything against the law?"

"You mean like stealing?"

"Yes."

He shook his head. "No. You just have to trust me, Savta," I leaned over and kissed him. "All right. No more questions, Matti," I said, but inside, my heart was heavy. Where did he disappear to and what did he do?

For the first weeks, he gave me no cause for concern at all. In fact, I was delighted. He walked with me to *The Pomegranate Pendant* every morning, helping me over the broken cobblestones with great solicitude. My failing eyesight did not allow me to make much jewelry these days, but Mattanyah's older brother Nissim had been my apprentice for three years and he did beautiful work, as beautiful as the jewelry his grandfather Ezra and his great-grandfather Djeddi had created in the same workroom. When we reached the store, he would spend a few minutes with his brother exchanging family news, run any errands that I needed, and then kiss me lightly and disappear for the rest of the day.

The truth is I had little time to worry about what he was doing. The Arabs were again resorting to unrestrained violence. Although we'd had relative quiet since the riots of seven years ago, now twelve Jews had been murdered.

The Jewish Agency was trying hard to prevent our young men carrying out reprisal attacks, but I knew it would only be a matter of time. The stony-faced British were always looking the other way when Jews were attacked and our original optimism that they would help us now seemed pathetically naive. In fact, they had become almost as much our enemy as the Arabs. They did little while our homes and institutions were pillaged and burned, while we were being brutally attacked – not only in Jerusalem, but wherever there were Jewish settlements. Nearly 4,000 Jews had been forced to leave their homes. Only when British lives and property were being threatened in Jerusalem did our new masters respond.

They had promised us so much, the British, with their Balfour Declaration. But our hopes had been pinned on a weak reed. They gave in to Arab pressure and did everything they could to prevent us from becoming a majority in the country. Each day we read in the papers of the terrible threat to our brethren in Europe with the rise of Nazism. Jews were arriving from Germany, Poland, Austria, Czechoslovakia, Hungary – all with terrible tales of anti-Semitism, oppression, arrests, and the threat to their existence. The problem was that even more Arabs had immigrated to Palestine since the Great War ended, drawn by the early security and stability of British rule. There was frightening talk that the British would heed the Arabs and prevent more Jews from coming, and this at a time when staying in Europe would mean certain death for them.

The Haganah tried to defend our settlements, and at the same time, to work for independence by means of political pressure and military restraint. But understandably, many Jews were impatient at the lack of progress and other resistance movements arose and took revenge when Jews were murdered and terrorized.

It was a time of great unrest in Palestine. Despite

the years of Sarah's tutelage, I felt I still knew little of politics, but Naomi, Sarah's widowed daughter who now lived in the apartment next door which had been her parents', became my instructress. The horrifying events that had befallen her family in Chevron had given her true insight into the nature of our enemy. Her youngest son Yitzchak had become friendly with my grandson since Mattanyah had moved in with me, and it gave me some comfort when they'd go off together, for I knew Yitzchak to be of a pious, stable nature.

"We must have our own homeland," Naomi would insist fervently.

"We will – when Mashiach comes," I would answer softly.

Like her mother, Naomi was full of fire. "We must help him to come. We can't sit back fatalistically waiting while Jews are being murdered every day."

I sighed. It was certainly written in the Torah. "To your descendants I give this Land from the River of Egypt to the Great River, the Euphrates..." Clearly we did not yet merit that gift. We would be satisfied with even less land, but the Almighty did not seem in a hurry to give us even what Lord Balfour had promised.

My children often tried to persuade me to leave the Old City, but my roots went deep. I loved it. Every alley had memories for me of my young husband, memories of my little ones, memories of Djeddi, and I felt that to leave would be like abandoning them. Still, I was often afraid. There were Arabs from whom I'd always bought vegetables, who used to be polite and even smile. Now these same vendors were sullen, their eyes reflecting hatred. They were secure in the knowledge that the British would not protect us, that their day would come.

Because there was a curfew, I always closed *The*

Pomegranate Pendant by mid-afternoon. Usually Mattanyah came and walked home with me. When he failed to show up one day, I was not overly perturbed. I was sure I would find him in the Chosh, either in his room or closeted with Yitzchak at Naomi's. However, he was in neither place.

Although I'd kept my promise and never went into his room, for some reason I felt uneasy. I turned the handle and was surprised to find the door unlocked. It was neat and clean and I was pleased. On the desk there was a box which I moved to see if perhaps he'd left a note for me. The box was surprisingly heavy. Curious, I opened it, and my heart stood still: inside was a gun and ammunition. Just then, I heard footsteps racing up the stairs and Matti burst in. He was white-faced with rage.

"What are you doing in my room? Just once I forgot to lock it and you come in, prying," he shouted.

"I was not prying. I was looking for you.

"In a box?"

I ignored the sarcasm. "You owe me an explanation. What are you doing with – this?" I couldn't even pronounce the word "gun," so hateful was it to me to see such a thing in my home.

"It is none of your business, Savta."

"Not my business! Have you killed someone? Am I sheltering a criminal?"

He laughed, but it was an ugly sound. "The British would say so."

I began to shiver. "You're training secretly with the Haganah?" I whispered.

"Not the Haganah." I waited, my heart thudding with fear. "They don't do enough. They fight their battles with words."

"Mattanyah, what are you saying?" I sat on the edge

of his bed, my hands trembling in my lap.

"I am with Etzel," he said proudly. "It would have been better for you – and for me – if you hadn't known, but you've asked and so I'm telling you." Etzel – *Irgun Tzva'i Leumi* – the militant resistance movement whose motto was "Fight Terror With Terror."

"No, Matti!" The words were wrung out of me. "It's not the way. You're just a boy..."

"Don't say that, Savta. I'm a man. I'm a soldier in the eyes of David Raziel!" I had heard of him, the Etzel Commander-in-Chief.

"Does he know your age, Matti?"

He pushed my hands away. "Many are younger than me."

A sudden thought struck me. "Is Yitzchak...?"

He nodded. "I recruited him. He has much to avenge – the murder of his father, his brother and his baby niece."

"Does Naomi know?" I asked tearfully.

He didn't answer. Then a new thought came to me. "Is Naomi involved?"

"Savta, you ask too many questions. Such knowledge is dangerous for you. The British have no pity on elderly Jews, even women like you. The less you know, the better for all of us." Even without his answer, I knew. Naomi, too, was an Etzel operative. I was suddenly glad Sarah had passed on, to be spared the fear that was cutting through me like a knife.

I started to cry. "You'll be caught. They will hang you." Etzel's exploits were in the newspaper every day: British flags taken down in secret and replaced with a Jewish one; telephone exchanges and railway lines blown up; reprisal attacks on Arabs...

Mattanyah put his arm around me. "If I die, Savta, I'll be a martyr, a hero. Even if it's short, my life will have had meaning. We must be masters of our own homeland – it must be a haven for Jews to come to from wherever they are being persecuted. Don't you understand, Savta?"

I understood, but I was desperately afraid for him. I, the old, the wise, buried my head on his shoulder and sobbed, while my sixteen-year-old grandson comforted me, his head filled with visions of a Jewish homeland that he might not live to see.

28

MATTANYAH continued to live with me, even after the house in Beit Hakerem was built. We helped each other: I was his alibi when he needed to explain where he was; he was my brawny protector and assistant. In truth I had come to depend on him. He had several narrow escapes when the British would come searching the house for contraband. Terrified as I was to have guns and ammunition in my home, I had found him safe hiding places for them. He worked at *The Pomegranate Pendant,* really just as a messenger boy, delivering goods to customers and collecting raw materials and supplies that we needed. It was a lowly occupation for the grandson for whom I'd had such ambitions, but it provided the cover he needed to move around Jerusalem with valid explanations whenever he was stopped by the British.

Because of his job, he could leave the Old City whenever he wished, and every day would find him at the Patt Bakery on the corner of Hanevi'im and Harav Kook Streets in the new city. He would stroll into the coffee shop like a regular customer, but, as soon as it was safe, he would disappear into a secret part of the building where there was an arms cache for the Haganah, and where Lechi and Etzel members also held meetings. Sometimes the British police and army were actually sipping coffee upstairs while the meetings took place in the basement or back rooms, and even leading Arab families, like the Nashashibis and Farrajes, would patronize the bakery without dreaming of the double role it played.

I was always afraid that Matti would be caught. I didn't worry too much about what would happen to me – I felt I'd lived my life – but he was still a boy with his whole life ahead of him. The White Paper of 1939 issued by the British, restricting Jewish immigration to 75,000 a year at a time when Jews were trying to flee Europe to save their lives, and giving the Arabs a veto on all Jewish immigration, removed my last objections to his activities. I was actually immensely proud of him. Eventually we took his father into our confidence, but not the rest of the family. Only then did we learn that Shalom was also working underground with the Haganah, which was less extremist than Etzel but also officially illegal. We had always been law-abiding citizens, in accordance with the Rabbinic injunction that "the law of the land is the law," but in such matters of life and death, where our people and our holy Land were in the balance, our loyalty lay on the side of our fellow Jews.

It was truly a dreadful period we were going through, and few families remained untouched. All our Yemenite friends living in Kfar Shiloach had to flee because of repeated Arab attacks. Reuven and Yifat and their large family moved at the same time that Shalom and Rina left for Beit Hakerem. They simply abandoned their houses and we helped them relocate to Nachalat Achim, a small suburb in the new city that had been founded fourteen years earlier. Everyone continued to press me to leave the Old City, but somehow I just couldn't do it. I lived with terror and tried to keep away from the Arab areas, where Jews were beaten daily and sometimes murdered under the uncaring eyes of the British.

Unbelievably, *The Pomegranate Pendant* supported

us all, even in these difficult times. Inside the store there were no politics, and there were British and Arabs as well as Jews among the customers. Naomi also helped out from time to time, dressing the window and acting as a saleswoman. We never discussed her frequent unexplained absences, and there was no need to. There was too much at stake.

While Hitler grew more and more powerful in Germany, western Europe closed its gates to Jewish refugees. The Holocaust piled horror upon horror, and the Jews had nowhere to go. Despite the dangers, boatloads of blockade runners called *"ma'apilim"* reached the coasts of Eretz Yisrael under cover of darkness. This wave of immigration was called *"Aliya Beit,"* for *bilti chuki* – illegal. Like Pharaoh in Egypt, the British had hardened their hearts towards the Jews. Their White Paper stated that the Jewish population of Palestine must not exceed one-third of the total population and that, after 1944, no Jews could immigrate without the permission of the local Arabs. It was a death sentence for any Jew who had managed to escape from Hitler's clutches, and the British fully intended to carry it out.

The *S.S. Patria,* carrying 250 refugees, was sabotaged; the 1,700 refugees on the *S.S. Atlantic* were exiled to Mauritius; the *S.S. Struma* was turned back and it was torpedoed in the Black Sea with all but one of the 769 souls on board lost. This cargo ship was meant for transporting cattle, yet the passengers – men, women and children – had been willing to risk their lives because they knew of the certain annihilation awaiting them in Romania.

Even after the war ended, while the smoke of the crematoria still blackened European skies, the British maintained their campaign to prevent Jews from landing in Palestine, and even intensified it. Hundreds of thousands of Jews who had been rescued from hell wandered the world in search of a haven, but even their own "national homeland" greeted them with closed doors. Ships were scoured for Jews before they left European ports. Aircraft searched them out at sea and shore patrol cutters hugged the coastline, while mounted troops waited on the shore for any immigrants who might succeed in landing despite the blockade.

Many nights Mattanyah, now a man of twenty-eight, was among those hiding on the deserted beaches to rescue the lucky ones who had managed to get through. In truth, I never knew exactly where my grandson went or what he did, but when I heard on the wireless or read in the papers of armed reprisals against Arabs, attacks on their buses, or of smuggling Jews into Palestine under the very noses of the British, I would tremble in fear of his arrest. Every knock on my door filled me with dread.

One night, however, a knock on my door brought an unexpected gift, in the form of a tiny immigrant waif. Mila was one of the illegal immigrants who had come on the *Af Al Pi* and Matti brought her to me to hide in my apartment. I at first thought her to be a child of no more than ten or twelve, for she was of very small build and terribly emaciated. In fact she was eighteen, a lovely but tormented girl with enormous pain-filled dark eyes. Mila's whole family had been wiped out in Poland. She suffered from horrid nightmares during the first few months, and I would hear her whimpering in her room like a beaten puppy. It was a heartbreaking sound.

Mattanyah was really taken by her – I was not sure if it was pity or love – and eventually they married. Although she was not Yemenite, I had grown very fond of her by then, and the marriage had my blessing as well as Shalom and Rina's. The couple continued to live with me and, in all honesty, during those dark days of fear in the Old City, I was glad for their companionship and protection.

Our family, may they all be protected from the Evil Eye, was growing at a great pace, and embracing many different ethnic cultures. *Baruch Hashem,* none had discarded their Jewish heritage or the mitzvot which I had learned from my dear parents in Sana'a and passed on to them, although some were more strict in their observance than others. We could count among us several outstanding Torah scholars, learning and teaching in Shomrei Ha-Chomot Yeshivah, which Rav Yosef Chaim Sonnenfeld had founded in Battei Ungarn. These scholars were a tremendous source of pride and our assurance of survival. Whatever our fate, the Holy Torah they learned and we cherished would never die. Assaf had led the way; his children and grandchildren, nephews and great-nephews had followed.

My daughter Ruchama was a leader too. Her sphere was *chesed.* Along with many of her religious friends, she helped raise money for Ezrat Nashim Hospital, which cared for the mentally ill. Without these very charitable women I don't know what might have befallen those unfortunate souls, including many war refugees whose minds were destroyed by the horrors they'd witnessed in Europe.

Shalom was the third pillar on which our family rested, the symbol of physical strength and the never-ending fight for justice for all Jews. I could see that same resolve in Mattanyah and his cousins.

While history continued to flow like a river in those dark and dreadful days of 1948, the Jewish calendar had its own uninterrupted rhythm that demanded our attention no matter what else was happening around us. As the month of Nisan approached, I begged my family to come to me for the Seder; I was eighty-one and felt it might be my last Pesach. At first they demurred: it would be too hard for me, it was dangerous in the Rova and so on, but I insisted. Some of them could sleep in Naomi's apartment next door and other neighbors in the Chosh had space to accommodate some of the children. The women would all cook and help in the preparations.

In the end, they agreed and it was arranged. It required a lot of organizing and my children took it upon themselves to make it a Seder night I would never forget. My daughter Ruchama and daughters-in-law Tirtza and Rina had divided the work among all my grandchildren and their children. My home had been cleaned from top to bottom and sparkled like a jewel. Amassing enough food had been a problem for it was very scarce, but we somehow managed it and the aromas wafting from the kitchen smelled tantalizingly delicious as we sat around the long tables we had setup in every room. Not only did we read the Haggadah and tell of the Exodus from Egypt, I also related the story of how I had left Yemen with my dear husband Ezra and how we had reached the Promised Land, and Mattanyah's wife Mila related a harrowing yet similar tale of the nightmare voyage, from Nazi Europe to Palestine and a new life.

Assaf, now a distinguished *Rosh Yeshivah*, regaled us with insights on the Haggadah text that brought the story to life. He told us that we must each regard ourselves as if we had personally experienced slavery in Egypt. To do this, he said, we needed to overcome dimensions of time, place and historical context. *Mitzrayim*, the Hebrew word for Egypt, has as its root *tzar,* he explained, "meaning narrow or constrained. To say that we must leave Egypt is to say that we must struggle to break out of our narrowness and free ourselves to attain our full spiritual potential." He stressed that the main lesson of Pesach is freedom – a concept so important that it is referred to in the very first of the Ten Commandments: *I am the Lord Your God, Who brought you out of the land of Egypt, out of the house of bondage.* "Only as free men and women can we fully observe the mitzvot."

"We *will* be free, you'll see," Matti insisted passionately. "We will break the yoke of British rule and be our own masters in Eretz Yisrael."

Shalom put his hand on his son's arm to quiet him, but Mattanyah shook it off. "The day is coming – and soon," he added vehemently. He indicated the matzot, piled on the snowy tablecloth. "Now we are eating the bread of affliction, but remember at the climax of the Seder we sing about the defeat of the Angel of Death."

It was not easy to rejoice on that night. There were light moments, when my littlest great-grandchild Amichai recited the *Mah Nishtanah* and the youngest children searched for and found the *afikoman.* I looked all around and thought, "Here we all are, 'the fruit of my loins,' gathered together in the Old City of Jerusalem, despite the Arabs who want to annihilate us and the British who want to subdue our spirit. They will never succeed, never! My children and others like them are our guarantee."

29

THE VOWS WE MADE
that Seder night were indeed
prophetic. A few weeks later, on May 16th,
1948, the last British troops left our shores and
the next day the State of Israel was born. But before
we barely had time to exult in the stirring event, the battle
for Jerusalem was joined. Arab armies invaded from the
south, east and north, and Tel Aviv was raided from the
air. The day after the United Nations' vote granting Israel
independence, Jewish settlements and main roads were
brutally attacked all over the country. In all, there were
seven Arab countries bent on wiping us out and pushing
our 600,000 Jewish citizens "into the sea."

The Seder night, with my family gathered around
me, had marked an end to many things. Now Jerusalem
was under siege. Water was so strictly rationed that we
re-used our dishwater for the garden, and baths became a
once-a-week luxury... just a sponge from a basin was all
we could manage. The only food Jerusalem saw came in
by armed convoy, and in the Old City, it was the most
serious: we were completely cut off from the rest of the
country

When the last of the British finally left in that fateful
May of 1948, and war officially broke out, there were
less than 2,000 of us left in the Jewish Quarter, mainly
old people like me, reluctant to pull up our roots, a few
children, and 200 young Jewish soldiers – including some
of my great-grandsons. The Haganah, now with
recognized status as the Israel Defense Forces, had posted

this small group of soldiers there to protect us, but they had few weapons with which to defend the Rova against the 33,000 Arabs who remained in the Old City.

The Arabs launched an attack on us a few days after war broke out, intent on slaughtering every Jew, but with the help of the Almighty, the soldiers and residents together managed to repel them. Peering through a crack in the heavy shutters, I could see youngsters in traditional Chasidic garb, barely bar mitzvah age, shouldering rifles taller than they were; and alongside them, women in head-kerchiefs hurling stones and bare-headed boys in short pants and sandals, taking aim with pistols.

Matti let me on a secret: the only piece of heavy artillery in Israel's armory during this time was the Davidka, a cannon that couldn't fire at all accurately but made a terrifying noise. Such a noise, in fact, that Iraqi troops who were in firm control of one section of Jerusalem heard it and fled, believing that we had some terrible weapon – maybe even an atomic bomb!

I enjoyed that story, but I had seen enough in my years to know that not every engagement with the enemy would end in victory.

Word filtered in to us about the tragedy at Kfar Etzion. I remembered meeting the citrus grove owner S.Z. Holzmann, who had acquired the land in 1935 and called it by a Hebraized version of his name. He had intended to set up a mountain holiday resort, but a year later, the Arab rebellion had brought his plans to a standstill. When a group of religious Polish Jews approached him five years ago with their idea to build a new settlement there, he happily gave them the land. Two more religious settlements were established there, to form Gush Etzion – the Etzion bloc. Gush Etzion settlers worked in afforestation, but most of their time was spent in defending the kibbutz from Arab attacks. Their years of bitter experience, however, did little to help them against the Arab legion.

Back in January a unit of thirty-five men from the Palmach and Haganah were sent to reinforce the Etzion bloc. They traveled on foot from Hartuv. Arabs intercepted them on the way, and killed every one of those valiant men. A relief convoy was sent in March, but they also suffered heavy losses.

And now, with Jerusalem under siege and unable to help the settlers, the Arab legion and vast numbers of Arab mercenaries tightened the noose on Gush Etzion. The kibbutzim were surrounded by tanks and heavy military equipment and it was clear that they could not hold out for long. The settlers had resolved to defend themselves to the last cartridge. "Everyone was asking, 'What is the latest news from Kfar Etzion?'" Matti told me. "Well, the final transmission came through by telegraph. Their last words were: '*Shema Yisrael Hashem Elokeinu Hashem Echad.*' They surrendered then, and the Arabs massacred all but three of them."

"*Baruch Dayan Ha-emet,*" I murmured, my eyes closed tightly to banish the thought that these would not be our last casualties.

Mattanyah reacted angrily. "No, Savta, we say that for those who die peacefully in their sleep, or after an illness, or even a sudden death. But men and women murdered by our enemies – their deaths must be avenged!"

"But not by you, Mattanyah," I pleaded. "God will avenge them. It is His work, not yours."

There seemed to be no end to our grief. The Arab Legion moved on from Gush Etzion to the Mount of Olives and, from there, bombarded the Rova day and night. Matti smuggled me out in an armed convoy just two days before the defenders surrendered. Our losses were terrible: 170 Jews had been killed and 1,000 injured by Arab shellfire, Even then, although I knew it was the only way to save my life, I sobbed that I didn't want to leave, but Matti and Shalom physically carried me out of my home in the midst of the firing.

"What of my store? What of *The Pomegranate Pendant?*" I cried hysterically.

"It is just a shop, Savta. Your life is worth more," Mattanyah insisted.

But he didn't understand. *The Pomegranate Pendant was* my life. Everything – good and bad – that had happened to me was tied up in it. It was my first home in the Holy Land. It was where my children were born and where my beloved husband had died. It was where Djeddi, my dear father, had created such beautiful jewelry and enriched our lives. It was more than a symbol: it was my soul I was leaving behind. As I was driven, for the last time, through the Ashpot Gate, like Lot's wife, I kept looking back. I was not turned to a pillar of salt, but I felt my limbs and my heart turn to lead.

No, it wasn't just the shop, I realized as the tears caked on my cheeks. It was Jerusalem, the city where King David had reigned, where the Holy Temple had stood and where the stones of the *Kotel* cried out to Jews in every corner of the earth to come and claim their heritage. I had no right to abandon my city.

I remembered then an incident that had taken place nearly fifteen years earlier. Rachamim, Assaf's son, was learning in Rav Kook's yeshivah at the time. There had been numerous cases of Jews being attacked by Arabs at the *Kotel* and countless complaints had been lodged with the Mandatory authorities. The Governor came up with what he thought was a brilliant solution to the problem, a "compromise" which he was convinced would satisfy both parties: the Jews would agree to relinquish their claim to the *Kotel,* and the Arabs would allow them to pray there unmolested. Knowing how stubborn Jews could be, he chose a clever approach: he went to see Rav Kook and presented his proposal, adding that Rav Sonnenfeld – who was the Rav of Jerusalem – had already accepted it. Then he presented his proposal to Rav Sonnenfeld, adding that Rav Kook, the Chief Rabbi of Palestine, had already accepted it.

Neither Rav believed for a moment that his colleague had done anything of the sort; however, they both knew that the Governor's scurrilous claim might have dire consequences. Each dispatched a student to deliver a message to his colleague. The students met by chance at the Mandelbaum Gate, and recognized one another. "My Rav did not agree!" they said in unison, then spun on their heels and hurried back to their respective yeshivot.

The Governor was quite taken aback when his plan completely backfired. Both *Rabbanim* responded with the same words: "Relinquish the claim to my *Kotel?* Never!"

I had abandoned my *Kotel.*

I went to stay in Shalom's beautiful house in Beit Hakerem, but found no comfort. I should have stayed in the Rova, I told myself again and again, even after I learned that all the men – residents, soldiers, the wounded, and even two women had been taken to Trans-Jordan as prisoners of war. The rest were evacuated to Katamon, a newly-captured suburb of southwest Jerusalem.

The Rova was ravished and plundered by the victorious Arabs. We didn't know the full extent of the damage, but we heard that they destroyed our magnificent synagogues. They also stole all my jewelry and burned

Chapter Twenty-Nine

The Pomegranate Pendant.

Who could think of the Old City without a single Jew left there? Seven centuries ago, the Ramban had discovered Jews living there. The old underground *beit knesset* of Yochanan ben Zakkai is reputed to have been there for 2,000 years, but now, like the once magnificent Churvah, it is in ruins. There were always Jews there...when it was conquered by the Selejuks and in the time of the Crusaders and of the Turks. I myself was there when the Turks left and General Allenby promised to be our beneficent ruler. And now, I too had abandoned it and all that it represented. It would have been better to have stayed and died there.

I was in torment, riven with guilt and sorrow. I searched for Psalms to comfort me: "Hear me when I call, O God of my righteousness... Hearken unto the voice of my cry, my King... Why stand You afar off, O Lord? Why hide Yourself in time of trouble?...I lift my eyes to the hills, whence comes my help..." but no answer came and there was no comfort. I cried in vain. I only knew that it felt like the Destruction of the Temple once again, the destruction of Jewish hopes and dreams for the future.

Finale

30

I HAD NEVER EXPECTED to live so long, for three score years and ten is the measure of man's days. Every day thereafter is considered a gift of God and my gift had been twenty years. And what a special gift it was: on this day, I would take part in the Chinah ceremony of my son Assaf's great grand-daughter, Bracha.

The intervening years since I left the Old City have been sad, even though great-great-grandchildren were born and now one of them was being married. My family established a new business – called *Gargush* – for I would not allow them to call it *The Pomegranate Pendant;* that name would die with me. We celebrated joyful occasions from time to time, but always we were aware that we could no longer visit the *Kotel.* Nor could I go to the Chosh where I had been happy, or even see the site of *The Pomegranate Pendant,* although I knew it was now just a heap of rubble.

Under the armistice agreement reached seven years ago, signed by Israel and Trans-Jordan, Jerusalem was divided from north to south, with several No-Man's Land areas delineated between them. Not only are we denied access to the Old City which is under Jordanian rule, and to the *Kotel* in spite of the Jordanian promise to the contrary; we have now heard that they built a road through the Mount of Olives cemetery, using the tombstones of our ancestors as paving stones. The Tomb of Shimon ha-Tzaddik has been converted into a stable and all the holy places desecrated.

Although Shalom tells me that the Sinai Campaign is virtually over as Israeli troops are within sight of the Suez Canal, there are still bloody battles. The two islands which block the Straits of Tiran will be the next to fall, and then the whole of the Sinai Peninsula will be occupied by Israel. Gamal Abd-el Nasser has announced that Egyptian forces are withdrawing.

I am weary in my soul, though I still have faith that one day the Old City and all that it enshrines will return to Jewish hands. I doubt if I will live to see it or the coming of Mashiach, although daily I await him. I dream sometimes that I am standing atop the Mount of Olives and there is a great throng, crying out: "David, King of Israel, long may he live!" In my dream, all the people I have known and loved are with me: my dearest mother, from whom I learned so much; Ezra with his coal black eyes and black beard still looking the same as the young bridegroom I had married; Djeddi with his hands full of jewelry he had created in precious gold and silver; my true and wise friend Sarah, my second mother, in her voluminous apron and sturdy black boots; my precious granddaughter Miriam...

But it is still just a dream. Sometimes my son-in-law Menachem takes me at midnight to Sha'arei Pinah on the main road where he lives in Meah She'arim. It is the meeting-place of the Yemenite Kabbalists. Although he is Ashkenazi, he has great respect for our traditions. He is a wonderful husband to my Ruchama, and I remember Djeddi's words: "He has the soul of a Yemenite." He takes me to the small women's section, and he sits with these dedicated souls who, in the small hours, read Yemenite prayers and delve into the mysteries of their Kabbalistic universe. They stay together until three o'clock in the morning and then, through the hushed streets, I go back to my daughter's house to sleep for a few hours before Menachem drives me back to Beit Hakerem. Shalom's house there is indeed lovely, surrounded by fir trees and perfumed flowers and bushes of jasmine.

Yet, why does my heart still pine for the dim, narrow streets of the Rova? They were broken and malodorous and often befouled by donkeys. Yet to me they were beautiful in a way impossible to describe. Perhaps because it is not a physical place. It is an emotion. a poem... a song... a prayer. And the *Kotel* is where the Divine Presence dwells.

There is a midrash about this ancient Wall from which the *Shechinah* has never departed. It rests there eternally, it is said, hovering in hidden and mysterious waves. Once Rabi Natan entered the Temple precincts and found the Holy Temple destroyed, all except the Western Wall, the *Kotel Ha-ma'aravi.* He asked what it was, and a man told him it was the place where the Divine Presence rests. He offered to prove it to Rabi Natan. He took an iron ring and fixed it to the wall and the ring started to sway to and fro. As he watched it, Rabi Natan saw the Almighty bowing down and mourning for the desolation of the *Beit Ha-mikdash* and for the exile of the Children of Israel. The Almighty is said to have pledged that the *Kotel* will never be destroyed.

Although I shall not live to see it, I know in my heart that Jews will again pray at the *Kotel* and build homes and lives in the Old City of Jerusalem. They will be sheltered as we once were by the great stone walls, and their souls will be free.

When the last resonating notes of the lively Yemenite music had died away, announcing the end of Bracha's

Chinah, she came to the corner of the garden where I sat, her face flushed from the dancing and radiant with happiness.

"Savta Mazal, thank you for lending me your pomegranate pendant. It's so beautiful. Help me unclasp it, please. I want to return it to you now."

"No, my dear," I said, "I want you to keep it."

"But why? Everyone knows you only lend it. That it is yours for your whole life. Please take it back."

She looked so innocent it made my heart ache.

"I am at the end of my life now, Bracha," I told her gently, "while you are just beginning yours. I am giving you a sacred trust. Every bride in the ben-Yichya family should wear it at her Chinah ceremony. I know many of them will not marry Yemenites but, perhaps out of respect for my memory, they will maintain the tradition. It is a very lovely one...the dab of henna representing a seal on the hand and heart. Tradition is very precious. No one should ever forget where they came from. Perhaps some think of us and our customs as primitive, but we are a proud people, clever and industrious. Djeddi used to jest that we Yemenites were modeled on the corpses resurrected in the Prophet Yechezkel's vision – the dry bones that fused together – for our bodies are slight and sinewy. We maintained the essence of all that was important and we had many pious sages, scholars and philosophers throughout the generations."

"But what of your necklace?"

"The pomegranate, with its many seeds, symbolizes fruitfulness," I explained. "I hope you will be blessed with many children, and that there will be many weddings in the family – not just of your children, but of all your cousins. I would like to think that you will pass it on and that my pomegranate pendant will be a talisman for good, for all the generations yet to come."

The Chinah ceremony had been held in the moonlit garden of Shalom and Rina's house. It was after midnight, and Shalom came to fetch me.

"Imma, come inside. It is very late and getting cold. See – the dew is falling."

I drew my shawl more tightly around my shoulders. "Not yet, my son. I want to sit here for a while and be as one with Jerusalem." A little dew wouldn't hurt a tough old woman like me.

I looked up through the branches and saw the stars shimmering like a million diamonds, the moon golden like my pomegranate pendant. I listened to the wind sighing in the fir trees that pointed like sentinels toward heaven. I inhaled the fragrance of a magnolia tree in the garden and rosemary, basil and thyme wafting down from the Judean hills...herbs that my mother had grown in Sana'a and I had planted in my tiny plot in the Chosh. I stooped and took a handful of soil and let it run between my fingers. I was saying goodbye to Jerusalem and had used all my five senses but one, in this silent dialogue with the city I loved. I hoped that Paradise would look like Jerusalem. And then, I tasted it – the salt of the tears that were slowly trickling from my eyes.

Ezra had been right from the start: we had come to Jerusalem to be redeemed. And so we were.

Glossary

The following glossary provides a partial explanation of some of the foreign words and phrases used in this book. The spelling and explanations reflect the way the specific word is used herein. Often, there are alternate spellings and meanings for the words. Foreign words and phrases which are immediately followed by a translation in the text or which have entered the English language and appear in recent dictionaries, are not included in this section.

ABBA: father; daddy.
ALIYAH: lit., ascent; immigration to the Land of Israel.
ARON KODESH: the holy ark in the synagogue which contains the Torah scrolls.
AVNEI MILUIM: the precious stones set in the High Priest's breastplate.

BEIT KNESSET: a synagogue.
BEIT MIDRASH: the study hall of a Yeshivah

CHACHAM: lit., "wise man," an honorary title for a learned man and community leader.
CHAG(GIM): Festival(s).
CHESED: compassion; lovingkindness.
CHINAH: a reddish-brown dye extracted from the leaves of the henna plant; the Yemenite pre-nuptial ceremony in which this dye is applied to the palms of the bride and groom.
CHOL HA-MO'ED: the intermediate days of the Festivals of Pesach and Sukkot.
CHUPAH: the wedding canopy; the wedding ceremony.

DERASHAH (-SHOT): sermon(s) or talk(s) on Torah subjects.

GAN EDEN: the Garden of Eden; the World to Come.

GEMATRIA: numerology; interpretation of the meaning of Hebrew letters and words through their numerical value.

HALACHAH: Jewish law.

IMMA: mother; mommy.

KASHRUT: the Jewish dietary laws.

KEHILLAH: a Jewish community or congregation.

KETUBAH: the marriage contract.

KIPPAH (-POT): skullcap(s).

MACHZOR(IM): prayer book(s) for the Festivals.

MARAK REGEL calves'-foot or leg of lamb soup.

MAZAL: fortune; lot.

MEZUZAH (-ZOT): rolled parchment(s) containing prescribed verses from the Torah, placed on door posts in Jewish homes.

MIKVEH (MIKVA'OT): pool(s) for ritual immersion.

MINYAN: a minimum of ten Jewish males aged 13 and over, the quorum required for congregational prayer.

MISHKAN: the Holy Tabernacle.

MORENU: "our teacher."

MORI: lit., "my teacher"; Yemenite title of respect for a Rabbi and teacher.

NUSACH ASHKENAZ: the Ashkenazic liturgical style and inflection.

PARNASSAH: livelihood.

RABBANIM: Rabbis.
RABBENU: our teacher; our master.

SEDER: the order of the Pesach night ceremony recalling the Exodus from Egypt and the liberation from bondage.
SHALIACH (SHELICHIM): emissary(ries); messenger(s).
SHUK: an open-air marketplace.
SIDDUR: the prayerbook.
SOFER: a scribe.
SUKKAH: a temporary booth lived in during the Festival of Sukkot.

TEHILUM: (the Book of) Psalms.
TZIYON: Zion; the Land of Israel.

YESHIVAH: an academy of Torah study.
YISHUV: the Jewish community in pre-State Eretz Yisrael.

Bibliography

Ben-Eliezer, Shimon 1975. *Destruction & Renewal The Synagogues Of The Jewish Quarter.* Jerusalem. Reuven Mass.

Collins, Larry and Lapierre, Dominique 1972. *0 Jerusalem.* New York. Simon and Schuster.

Efrati, Nathan 1982. *Homecoming.* Jerusalem Kollek & Son.

Gerlitz, Menachem 1979. *The Heavenly City.* Jerusalem/New York. Feldheim Publishers.

Gilbert, Martin 1977. *Illustrated History Atlas.* Jerusalem. Steimatzky.

Halper, Jeff 1991. *Between Redemption and Revival.* Boulder Colorado & Oxford U.K. Westview Press.

Katz, Emanuel 1987. *Lechi: Fighters for the Freedom of Israel.* Tel Aviv Friedman Publishers.

Laqueur, Walter 1972. *A History of Zionism.* New York/Chicago/San Francisco. Holt, Rinehart and Winston.

Lusin, Yigal 1982. *Pillar of Fire.* Jerusalem. Shikmona.

Muchawsky-Schnapper, Ester *Iconography & Interpretation in Yemenite Jewelry.* Ethnography Dept. Israel Museum Encyclopaedia Judaica.

Schwester, Selma 1974. *My Life and Experiences at Shaare Zedek* as told to Trude Fraenkel, from hospital archives.

Sonnenfeld, S.Z. 1989. *Anashim Shel Tzurah.* Jerusalem. Hed Press.

Vilnay, Zev 1973. *Legends of Jerusalem.* Philadelphia. Jewish Publication Society.

– A Sequel To The Pomegranate Pendant –

Seeds Of The Pomegranate

Lightning Source UK Ltd.
Milton Keynes UK
UKOW03f2132250314

228824UK00001B/79/A